D0998909

BOOKBINDING
Techniques and Projects

Josep Cambras

DECORATIVE TECHNIQUES

BARRON'S

BOOKBINDING
Techniques and Projects

Contents

chapter 2
TOOLS AND MATERIALS

TOOLS AND MATERIALS

- Machinery, 24
  Sheer
  Guillotine
  Plough
  Book Press
  Backing Press
- Tools, 26
- Materials, 29

chapter 1
HISTORY AND EVOLUTION

BRIEF HISTORY

- The Origins, 10
  Mesopotamia
  Egyptian Papyrus
- The Development Period, 12
  The Codex
  Paper
  The First Covers
  The Development of the Cover
- The Classics, 14
  The Invention of the Printing Press
  New Solutions for Covers
- The Modern World, 16
  Mass-Produced Bindings
  Art on Mass-Produced Bindings

**NEW MATERIALS
AND NEW INSPIRATION**

- New Materials . . . , 18
- . . . and New Inspiration, 20

chapter 3

PROCESSES AND TECHNIQUES

SEWING

- Sewing Loose Sheets, 34
- Sewing a One-Page Signature, 35
- Sewing a Multiple-Page Signature, 36
- Exposed Sewing, 37
- Sewing with Ribbons, 38
- Japanese-Style Sewing, 39

GLUING

- Making Adhesive Paste, 40
- How to Prepare the Mixture, 41
- Rubber Cement, 41
- The Paper Fibers, 42
- Preparing Ordinary Fabric, 43
- Gluing the Pastedowns, Headbands, and Spine, 44
- Double Layering, 45
- Inserting a Ribbon, 45

CUTS AND FOLDS

- Cutting Paper and Boards, 46
- Folding and Finishing Borders, 47
- Cuts and Folds in a Box, 50
- Compartments in a Tray, 51
- Two Types of Lids, 52
  Attached Lid
  Detached Lid
- Scoring, 54
  Accordion
  Cardboard Case for Books

PROJECTS AND DECORATION

- How to Make a Cushioned Surface, 56
- How to Paint the Ends of Books, 57
- Several Cover Samples, 57
- Window to Hold a Picture, 58
- Texture with Newspapers, 60
- Paper Cutouts, 61
- Decorating with Juxtaposed Papers, 61

SIMPLE RESTORATIONS

- Reconstructing the Spine, 62
- Loose Covers and End Papers, 64

chapter 4

PAPER PAINTING TECHNIQUES

PAINTING PAPER

- How to Paint Paper with Repeated Motifs, 68
- Marbleized Paper, 70
- Painting Paper with Wax, 72
- Crumpled Paper and Salt Paper, 74
- Paper Painted with Paste, 76
- Painting Paper by Folding, 78

chapter 5

STEP-BY-STEP PROJECTS

- Portfolio with Flaps, 82
- Journal and Case, 86
- Travel Journal, 90
- Bradel-Binding Booklet, 94
- Photo Album, 97
- Book with Ribbons and Exposed Sewing, 100
- Book with Flap and Closure, 102
- Japanese-Style Book, 106
- Box with a Detached Lid, 108
- Continuous Protective Case, 112
- Case in Book Format with Flat Spine, 116
- Case in Book Format with Round Spine, 122
- Pencil Case, 128
- Picture Frame, 130
- Magazine Holder, 132
- CD Holder, 134
- Puzzle, 138

GLOSSARY, 142

Introduction

The goal of this book is to introduce the reader to the world of bookbinding through a series of methods and techniques. As a teacher, I realize the difficulty involved in creating a piece because of lack of knowledge of the subject matter, for fear of making a mistake, or for other reasons. This is why this book is so important: it will acquaint the reader with a series of easy steps from the beginning.

The book consists of several chapters that culminate in the creation of a final piece.

We begin this process by referring to history because the desire to protect, and at the same time enhance, the beauty of any written or printed document has existed since ancient times. But times change, and with them so do the materials and methods that are used for this activity; and this is the foundation of future new techniques.

The second chapter provides a list of small tools and various materials for creating the first projects. The third chapter introduces the techniques, methods, and the practical knowledge needed to work with the materials.

In the next chapter, the different approaches for painting paper are reviewed briefly. The last chapter includes projects that the reader can work on while reading them. The content of this book corresponds to one of the two courses recommended for the first year of studies in bookbinding. We are confident that it will help the reader establish a good foundation to get started in this fascinating world with endless possibilities, enjoying each moment and each exercise without the need for an elaborate workshop or studio.

Josep Cambras
Bookbinding Professor at the Escuela
d'Arts I Oficis of the Diputación of Barcelona

History and Evolution

Paper objects and similar devices (CDs, DVDs, etc.)
are an important part of the things that we all tend to
collect and that we use all the time, today and always.
This is why there is the need for organizing, protecting,
and personalizing the objects, especially those that are
most important.
In this chapter, we try to offer a timeline of its bookbinding's evolution. We explain it in general terms, through the
most representative objects of the different eras, while of-
fering some ideas that can serve as inspiration when you
encounter a similar problem. Obviously, the goal is not
to imitate the models but to offer ideas that could help
solve similar issues, with other materials, in a different
time period, and with different taste.

Brief History

From the beginning of time, humans have had the irresistible desire to decorate or to embellish the objects they used on a daily basis. Also, the need developed early in history to protect certain objects or materials that were subject to deterioration over time. This is why innumerable possibilities were developed over centuries to create pieces that brought together the practical and the esthetic and that were limited only by people's imaginations.

The Origins

In this book we explain the changes that some techniques have experienced through time. Obviously, this is not intended to be a comprehensive explanation of their development but a point of reference, and especially a point of inspiration, for those who encounter problems similar to the ones described. We will focus mainly on written documents or paper objects; their predecessors, substitutes, and similar objects form the body of the projects presented in this book.

The oldest known documents must be protected, and it must be done in such a way that esthetic value is added to the purely practical. However distant the culture may seem, we find sophisticated systems for storing, protecting, and decorating documents from the beginning of recorded history.

Document on clay. Ancient cuneiform writing tablet from Mesopotamia (Third Millennium B.C.E.)

Cuneiform writing tablet made of clay with a protective casing also in clay.

Mesopotamia

In Mesopotamia (present-day Iraq), clay was used as a support for writing since the Fourth Millennium B.C.E. A wedged stick was used to write on these clay tablets. With time, this gave way to cuneiform writing, the oldest form of writing known. By then, an interesting system had already been invented to protect some of the valuable documents. The tablet, which was made of clay, was inserted inside a clay casing for protection. This invention required a certain degree of experience and sophistication.

In other words, we are looking at one of the first document protection devices. This is an extremely original solution for the challenging task of protecting a document, made with the same material.

Egyptian Papyrus

Later, new supports and writing systems were developed. The main innovations were the extraordinary Egyptian papyrus—the parchment paper used since ancient times but made popular by the Greek city of Pergamon, after which it was named—and the different types of wood and wax tablets used a little bit in every period.

Papyrus was an aquatic plant that grew abundantly in the marshes and swamps of the Nile River. In the early days, the Egyptians discovered a way to transform it into a very useful material for writing. This is the closest predecessor of our paper, whose name comes from the word *papyrus*. When this excellent material was available, the Egyptians had to figure out how to store it and protect it. They devised some of the most diverse and creative techniques. Sometimes they folded the papyrus pieces to prevent them from wearing out while being transported, but they rolled them as well. This method of storing was also applied to parchment paper and to documents written on long and soft materials, such as leather, and has been used commonly in different

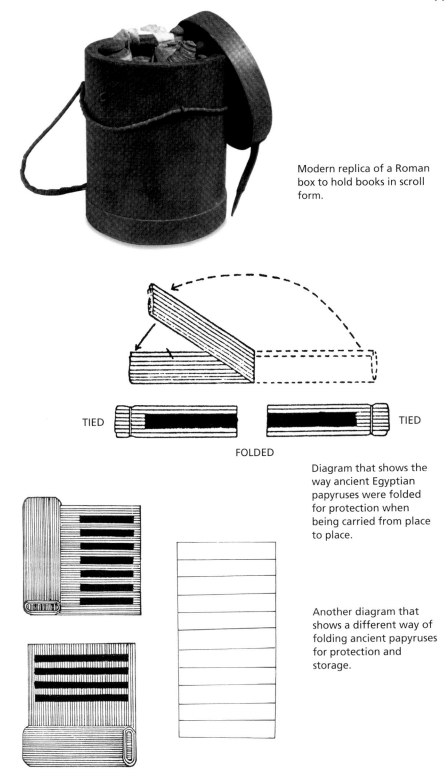

Modern replica of a Roman box to hold books in scroll form.

TIED   FOLDED   TIED

Diagram that shows the way ancient Egyptian papyruses were folded for protection when being carried from place to place.

Another diagram that shows a different way of folding ancient papyruses for protection and storage.

periods. Magnificent boxes were constructed from various materials to protect and carry the pieces without causing any damage. Most of these boxes were made of wood or leather, but others were made of more precious materials and with more elaborate decorations, if their contents were considered important or valuable. An interesting variation is the box that traditionally served to store and carry the Judaic legal books in the form of scrolls.

The Development Period

After numerous trials and innovations spanning centuries, a period of development began marking the transition to the printed book and classic binding. This period takes place during the Middle Ages, and religious books are its main protagonists.

The Codex

During the Middle Ages the form of documents changed substantially. In fact, during this period forms similar to the ones we know today first emerged. Two main changes took place at this time. On the one hand, what is technically known as the codex, the document with the form of the present-day book, made its appearance. It consisted of a series of pages bound at the spine with a cover that was more or less elaborate depending on the importance of the particular document. This is not only the format of present-day books, but also of pads, folders, and a wide range of other modern stationery products.

Metal protectors for an Italian medieval binding. Heavy metal pieces have been added to a sheet of wood covered with leather to protect and decorate the book.

Paper

The second great innovation of this period was paper, which had a form very similar to the paper we know today. The secret of its production surfaced in China and expanded to the West through the Arab world. They learned the Chinese techniques and then modified and improved them. These new techniques spread throughout the Mediterranean countries around the tenth century A.C.E. Only later did these techniques spread into Christian Europe.

With both discoveries, we come close to the forms that we know today. The codices, that is, the book in its present-day form can be made of various materials, mainly parchment or paper, with numerous technical and decorative innovations, incorporated in both cases.

The modern concept of "binding," that is, the outside of a book, the covers with a dual purpose, had emerged. On the one hand, these covers protect and preserve what is inside, and on the other, they dignify it and enhance it, allowing it to be carried and read while holding it together.

The First Covers

The first known books (codices) are religious books. Many of them have what is referred to as "altar binding", in other words, covers that are often made of wood with a gold veneer and with pre-

A Mudejar-style Spanish binding from the sixteenth century. The technique consists of a decorated pressed leather cover on cardboard.

cious and semiprecious materials embedded in them.

The ornamentation was done to make the covers valuable and at the same time artistic, in accord with the sacred pages bound inside of them. Since bookbinding's origins and throughout the Middle Ages, many types of book covers made their appearance in response to the different forms and needs. Later, book covers played a role in the development of these art objects, which are used as a source of inspiration to this day.

Various protective devices were created. They were generally made of wood covered with leather, cloth, metal, or some other suitable material. This type of individual and durable wood box made the identification of the document possible and at the same time helped to protect it; oftentimes, this structure was reinforced with metal hardware used for protective purposes or as a latch. It also provided ample margin for creativity when it came to decoration.

In some cases, the book itself could be protected with a wood box, which was embedded ornamental pieces and even decorated with cloth or leather. The leather cover could be decorated with engraved motifs or iron stamping. These decorations were especially relevant in the Islamic world and had a spectacular development in the Iberian Peninsula, with the Mudejar binding, whose decoration was linked to the traditional leather craftsmanship of the East.

The Development of the Cover

Other types of decorations were made of fabric or precious cloth, very characteristic of the Byzantine world. They could be painted or have a very simple parchment cover. Or they could have wood covers with all kinds of decorative motifs (metal, engravings, etc.). Another innovation was envelope binding, a binding technique specific to the Muslim world. It was commonly used, especially for the documents used on ships. This type of binding, generally light, consisted of an envelope-like fold that made it possible to keep the piece closed and protected with a cord or a tie.

Cover to protect a book belonging to the Spanish Catholic monarchs (fifteenth century). It consists of a blue velvet jacket with enamel appliqués.

Exterior decoration of a sixteenth-century Persian book. It has been decorated with a painting technique on a leather cover.

Decoration inside of a sixteenth-century Persian book cover. A painting technique has been used, but this time on paper.

The Classics

Beginning in the fifteenth century, the world of books experienced a real revolution. With the development of the printing press two intimately related phenomena emerged: mass production and, consequently, the need for individualization. In general terms, this period, defined as semi-industrial, spans well into the nineteenth century, at which time the industrial production becomes widespread.

The Invention of the Printing Press

Up until this point, each book or document was a unique piece, even if it was a copy of the same original. Since books were made by hand, they were without a doubt the handiwork of craftsmanship and could not be replicated. On the other hand, books were scarce. Each piece depended on the ability and resources of its author, who contributed his distinctive hallmark. From the moment the printing press was born, it was possible to produce a large number of pieces that were almost identical. Only if the owner wished to add original elements was differentiation or individualization possible. The book was no longer individualized as it had been previously. Besides, there were a greater number of books, which increased the need for differentiation. From this moment on, we see the birth of different categories of books, depending on their characteristics. Books that did not change their original appearance represented the most common types and can be classified as the dull machine-made products. Then, there are those books that are bound for practical reasons and without much care for esthetics, generally with boards and parchment covers, or parchment alone. Finally, we come to the documents that are coveted by owners who want to turn them into unique objects, with more or less elaborate and valuable elements. This is the group in which we are especially interested.

The inside of a Turkish binding from the nineteenth century. Marbleized paper is the decorative element inside.

Another example of a Turkish binding from the middle of the nineteenth century, using marbleized paper for the interior.

Detail of the construction process of a modern handmade binding.

New Solutions for Covers

The various solutions that were developed responded to different objectives. Generally, the decorative forms had less variety than in previous periods, but later they would be imitated until today. In fact, these solutions developed into what is referred to as the classical decoration.

In general, excessively heavy wood covers were abandoned and replaced by boards covered with leather and, later, with decorated papers that were used for the exterior as well as endpapers. So, a standard was created for decorated books, all leather, half-bound leather, and cardboard or paper. The all leather ones are the most elaborate, but they belong to the group of artistic binding that is not covered here. Their decorations can be extremely complex; they may have gold appliqués, small metal elements, fragments of bound leather (mosaic), or simply stamped patterns.

But there are other simpler options for decorating covers. On the one hand, the surface of the board or the leather can be painted. In fact, this technique was often used in the Islamic world and was also seen in the West. A similar solution is provided by using marbleized paper, which was very popular in Ottoman Turkey. Because of its great esthetic value, it can be used as pastedown, as a cover, or as a separate decorative element.

An interesting variation of this technique is the Spanish and Valencian book cover bindings, which were produced in Spain between the eighteenth and nineteenth centuries with a technique similar to that of marbleized paper.

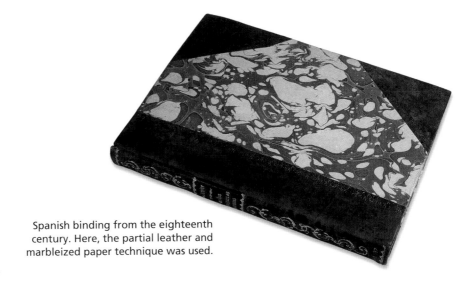

Spanish binding from the eighteenth century. Here, the partial leather and marbleized paper technique was used.

Spanish book from the first quarter of the nineteenth century. It is a *Foreigners' Guide* with a painting decorating the cover.

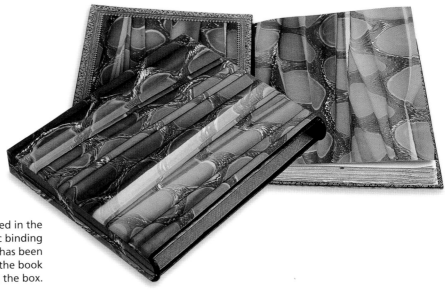

A bibliophile's book and box constructed in the twenty-first century following classic binding techniques. The same marbleized paper has been used for decorating the interior of the book and the box.

The Modern World

The main characteristic of this era is the dominance of the industrial revolution. It was almost impossible to individualize products, and even those that had been handmade were now produced on a machine. Obviously, these products have greater popular appeal because they are less expensive and often more practical, but they do not possess the quality and uniqueness of those produced in earlier times.

Mass-Produced Bindings

In general terms, during the twentieth century the art world followed one path while machine-made products followed another, at least in terms of bookbinding. Even though it is true that craftsmanship never disappeared completely, its place was relegated to machine-made products. Also, there emerged a variety of new materials as well as a new mentality based on consumerism and quantity over quality, probably with a focus on supplying products for everybody rather than providing selected and quality pieces to a few. The process has been growing slowly but surely, experiencing both setbacks and periods of rapid growth.

Mass-produced binding in paper, cardboard, cloth, and later plastic materials dominated a great part of the nineteenth and twentieth centuries, when publishers were pressured by the need to provide products that were less expensive. Bindings that were not of bibliophile quality were often used only for protective purposes, with no regard for esthetics, the same way that class notes or a book that is used often would be. For example, schoolbooks that were used all the time without concern for protection were lined with plastic or self-adhesive covers.

On the other hand, the widespread expansion of photography and printed material became the ideal decorative solution for most book covers, including the obvious development of the book jacket as a true binding element and main ornamental motif.

Art on Mass-Produced Bindings

Some machine-made products have reached an artistic quality that imitates the ancient techniques and craftsmanship, but these periods are almost always very specific and do not last long. Certainly, we miss the old artistic quality and attempts have been made to combine technology and the old values (the Arts and Crafts, Modernism, and Art Deco movements are clear proof of it) without making it a widespread phenomenon. For a long time, machine-made finishes were popular among most consumers. In fact, the industry tried to satisfy their taste to sell more.

At the same time, the arts made incredible advances, but often these had little to do with the processes, with mass-produced items, and even with the taste of the time. Each world had its own priorities and objectives, and it was difficult to make them both meet.

In any event, the philosophy in the modern world is to replace frequently the objects that are no longer popular. Quantity is oftentimes preferred to

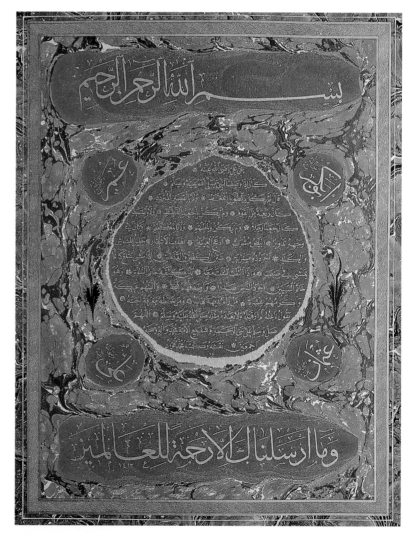

Modern example of a decorative technique in calligraphy on marbleized paper.

quality. The use and enjoyment of products (like books), which before were only accessible to a minority, has become widespread. Everybody has access to them at a very affordable price. The arts play a major role in creating the appeal and appearance of these products, but that influence generally reflected an industrial standpoint and was usually aimed at the masses, who were the focus of the industry. Personal taste seemed to be at odds with the concept of mass production.

Modern mass-produced box to protect and keep together two volumes of the same work.

Modern handmade binding in folder format to protect and personalize a book.

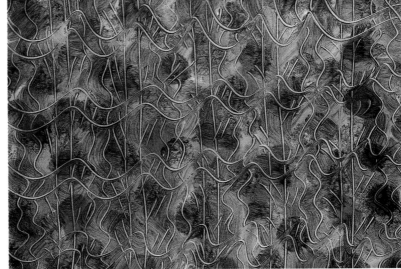

Work by Malevich, where very simple elements provide a magnificent result.

Modern decoration made by hand with mixed techniques, which include engraving.

New Materials
and New Inspiration

Nowadays there are many products and devices to store information. Some are reminiscent of the classic book shape (cassettes, CDs, video tapes, DVDs, etc.), whereas others present a challenge and have a similar shape and function (journals, folders, pamphlets, notes, etc.) All these new types of documents require some decorative or personalization element, the same way books did at the time of their inception.

New Materials . . .

New types of materials that were unthinkable in the past, like plastics, have emerged. They are a departure from the traditional paper and present new challenges. In general, protection for these types of books has been entrusted to industry or can be made in an easy and inexpensive way. Therefore, this is no longer the most important problem requiring our attention. However, the need to personalize objects is perhaps more appealing than ever before because of the great number of products available and the saturation of strictly mass-produced items and their consequent rejection by large numbers of people. This probably explains the increasing desire and need for personalizing things.

Today we not only have the resources needed but also models that can be

Another example of a modern mass-produced piece reminiscent of a book. It is a plastic box to protect and identify a commercial DVD.

A compact disc with a mass-produced case that allows the insertion of a booklet with the lyrics of the songs.

Plastic box for a modern videotape. It facilitates storage and helps identify the contents while protecting the delicate tape.

used as references. It is a very personal choice, as it should be, but twenty-first century art provides new models and new styles that should be added to the classic repertoire as sources of inspiration. The range of possibilities and styles to follow is greater than ever before. It is difficult to find somebody who does not identify with a specific look or style and who does not want to be surrounded by products that reflect his or her own taste.

Also, the artistic development of recent years has provided many new techniques and materials that can be used in the decoration of our favorite objects. If artistic binding has generated interesting advances in this area, the possibilities for personalizing covers, boxes, and the like can be endless. We will show some of them in this book.

Detail of a decoration in *pique assiette* (mosaic with tile shards) by Antonio Gaudí.

Mondrian shows the possibilities of combining geometric shapes.

Work by Miró. Mixed decorative techniques.

. . . and New Inspiration

Recent art techniques have been used spontaneously to decorate or personalize a variety of objects. They are even common in regular bindings, which are given an individual look whether they are for commercial, business, or personal use. Collage is probably the easiest and most widespread form of decoration, which best allows the expression of creativity. It was used repeatedly in twentieth-century art by Picasso, Braque, Miró, and Tàpies, among others. Drawing, photography, and color painting can be mixed in this medium; it also allows the use of pieces from other documents, like newspapers and similar graffiti tech-

The extreme simplicity of Malevich can be an effective source of inspiration.

Work by Tharrats, where the artistic possibilities of simple brushstrokes are illustrated.

niques. However, other twentieth-century artistic techniques can be used as inspiration for modern decoration (e.g., Gaudí's *pique assiette* or the mixed techniques used by a great number of contemporary authors).

Broadly speaking, twentieth-century art values creativity over technique and individualism over the subscription to specific styles and movements. It favors personalization, which is beginning to be considered an essential part of life and of modern objects, as opposed to domination by the industrial process and mass production in all of its aspects. It is therefore an invitation to develop one's own personality by exercising the creative processes like the ones proposed here.

Franz Marc preferred the bold use of colors and shapes.

Poster by Miró. It is based on the use of photographs in a collage.

Work by Arp, which creates volumetric effects.

2

Tools and Materials

The tools used for bookbinding are divided into two groups: large tools, especially machinery, and small tools. The latter include the small devices that help us in the process and that can often be substituted for larger machines, although they cannot be compared when it comes to the time needed to complete the work.

Tools and Materials

Historically, the tools and materials used in bookbinding are very similar to those that exist today, although their functionality and precision have been improved. Thanks to new technologies, a large variety of adhesives are available on the market; they complement those that have been traditionally used. The same is true for papers and other materials for making books and similar objects; nowadays there are many types and prices available.

Machinery

Of the machines used for binding books, we are going to discuss the smaller ones that can be used at home or in small studios on the following pages. They provide the same precision and results of the larger ones, but they are not suitable for large schools or large shops.

Sheer

Basically, the sheer is used for cutting sheets of paper and boards. It works like a pair of large scissors; one of its blades is attached to a surface while the other is movable because it has an axis at one of its ends. Large sheers are available, but a simple tabletop one is sufficient for small projects. It has one guide in the front and one in the back, parallel to the cutting line, which helps make parallel cuts, and a guide on either side, which is perpendicular to the sheet and helps make 90-degree cuts. It is mainly used to remove frayed edges, to even out papers and boards, to cut strips of paper, and so on.

Guillotine

The guillotine is very practical for cutting large stacks of paper. It has a blade that comes down vertically and diagonally to the plane. Guillotines come in many sizes. Tabletop guillotines can be operated manually with a wheel or with a lever; electric ones are used where safety concerns are greater because they require both hands to activate different switches. They are equipped with a pressure bar that drops down from above to hold the paper in place. The backstop, which is parallel to the blade, can be moved up or down with a handle. They usually come with a side guide as well to help make square cuts. The book or the stack of papers has to be held tightly against the guides to make sharp, precise cuts.

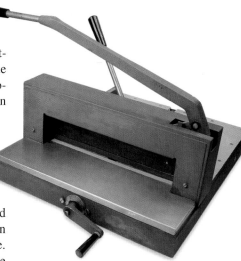

Guillotine.

Sheer.

Plough.

Book press.

Plough

The plough is used instead of the guillotine to trim books. It is a small press fitted with a blade that slides along guides. These are located on the lower part of the press; therefore, the press must be turned over to make the cut. It is a good idea to have a board with a square to make sure the cuts are made correctly.

Book Press

The book press is the most common tool in the process of binding books and journals. It is made of iron, and its two planes come together and separate thanks to a screw that moves the top plate while keeping the bottom one stationary. Two side guides allow the upper element to move fairly evenly. To use it, we suggest placing the paper between two wood boards so it does not come in direct contact with the metal.

Backing Press

The backing press is another basic tool in the bookbinding shop. It is practical for different processes, although for the exercises presented in this book it will be used to make the various cuts to sew the spine. It can work as a book press by placing it vertically and using two wood boards.

This is a horizontal press attached to two guides and a central axis, which sets one of its surfaces in motion. It should be installed on a four-legged wood base that is open in the middle.

Backing press.

Tools

All the tools used in the bookbinding shop deserve special attention: they must be cared for, cleaned, sharpened, and maintained in good working condition to guarantee a good finish for the work. There should be a designated place for each tool so they can be handy at all times and in proper working condition in case they are needed.

• Saws

You should have saws of various thicknesses to prepare the books for sewing.

• Rasps

Rasps are used to polish the sides of the boards and to give them a padded feeling.

• Scissors

Scissors are used for cutting paper and the sewing thread. They come in different sizes; however, it is better to use conventional scissors without ergonomic handles like the ones used in offices. Scissors with ergonomic handles cannot produce certain cuts where flat scissors are needed.

• Rulers

Rulers from 12 to 20 inches (30 to 50 cm) in length are very important for measuring and can also be used as straight edges for cutting. They are usually flat and made of metal.

• Divider

The divider is a tool that has two movable legs that end in points. It has a screw, which is used to measure and must be approximately 6 inches (15 cm) high. It is used for measuring and marking distances.

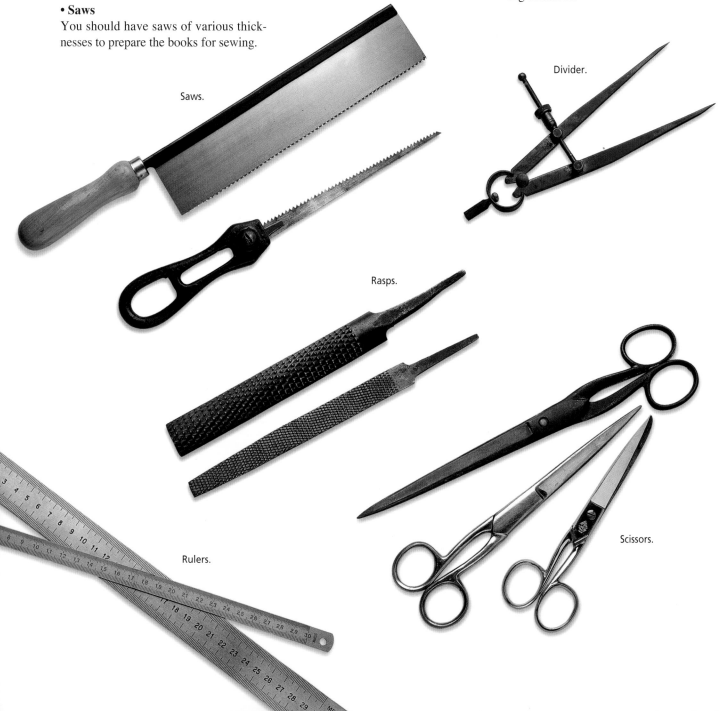

Saws.

Divider.

Rasps.

Rulers.

Scissors.

• Hammer
A hammer is a square or round iron mallet. Basically, it is used for rounding off the signatures and for evening out the thickness of the board.

• Awl
An awl is a thick needle attached to a wood handle. It is used to make holes in boards or papers.

• Weight
Weights are essential for pressing the signatures or the boards after they have been glued. They are available with handles so they can be held comfortably. Any object with a flat side and a certain amount of weight can be used for this purpose.

• Bone Folder
The bone folder is a vital tool for the bookbinder. It can be made of wood, bone, Teflon, and even plastic, although the latter two are not recommended. It is normally used to fold and score paper during the entire binding process.

• Craft Knife or Scalpel
The scalpel is used to cut and scrape, just like a small knife. It is frequently used in the bookbinding shop and comes with various tips depending on the work it is intended for.

Awl.

Bone folders.

Utility knives and scalpel.

Hammer.

Weight.

• Brushes

Brushes come in various thicknesses and sizes and can be used for small tasks like repairing a small tear and for larger ones like applying glue to a piece of cloth or to a large sheet of paper. They should be of good quality so they do not shed any bristles. It is a good idea to soak them in water for twenty-four hours before using them for the first time.

• Sandpaper

Either in sheets or attached to a wood support, sandpaper can be used to polish the different finishes. They are available in different numbers according to their coarseness.

• Spine Rounding Form

The spine rounding form is a wooden device that has half-round channels of different sizes. It can be used to form the cardboard used to make the book's spine.

Brushes.

Sandpaper.

Spine rounding form.

Materials

Like the tools, the materials also have to be kept in good condition. It is important to have adequate space to store them, and also to keep the papers clean and well organized in folders ready for use.

• Rubber Cement
Rubber cement is used only occasionally, in few specific instances to glue various materials, in addition to paper and cardboard.

• Adhesive Spray
Adhesive spray is also available to glue photographs. It is clean and has the advantage of not making the paper buckle when being used.

• Polyvinyl Acetate
Commonly known as bookbinding plastic glue, polyvinyl acetate is very useful for gluing different materials. It can be diluted with water and at the same time mixed with methylcellulose to give it a different consistency (see section on glues).

• Thread and Cord
Thread and cord are used for sewing, and they can be made of nylon or vegetable fibers; in the latter group, hemp and linen are the most common. They can be used for sewing, holding things together, although sometimes they can also be part of a decorative element.

• Headbands
Headbands are used to protect and, at the same time, to decorate. Some are handmade, but there are many available to choose from at affordable prices.

Rubber cement.

Adhesive spray.

Polyvinyl acetate.

Thread and cord.

Headbands.

Ribbons.

• Ribbons

All types of ribbons are very useful for making folders and booklets. They are available in cotton, silk, satin, and in different colors and sizes.

• Elastic Bands

Elastic bands are very practical for making folders and boxes and are sold in fabric stores. A hole has to be made on the board with a **punch** and finished with a **metal grommet**.

• Color Pencils and Markers

Pencils and markers are very useful to touch up small mistakes on the paper or in a corner of the board when it is covered.

• Paints

Such paints, acrylic, oil, and gouache, are used to cover a wide range of papers with different techniques and procedures.

• Binding Cloths

Binding cloths usually have a paper backing on one side, which makes gluing much easier. There are many wonderful catalogs that offer a great selection.

• Binding Boards

Binding boards usually come in two formats: Davey board and two-ply conservation board. In the exercises in this book, we will primarily use the conservation board since it is lighter and can be cut more easily; also, it does not buckle as readily.

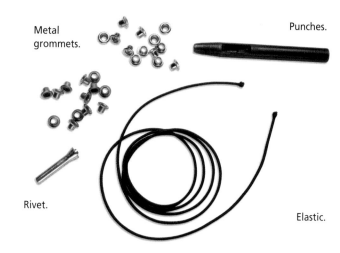

Metal grommets.

Punches.

Rivet.

Elastic.

Binding cloths.

Color pencils and markers.

Binding boards.

Painted papers.

• Painted Papers
Painted papers are available in many colors and are used to decorate the objects created. Some of them are handmade, but the ones with patterns are machine made.

• Corrugated Board
Corrugated board has many applications. It can be placed over another cardboard and be easily folded, and it can also be used by itself as a folder or booklet because of its consistency.

• Japanese Paper
This very textured paper comes in many colors and weights, so that it can cover a great variety of objects.

• Special Papers
In addition to the papers and boards previously mentioned, a large assortment of paper is available in commonly used colors, textures, and weights. They can be very useful, for example as the background of a painted paper.

Special papers.

Japanese paper.

Corrugated board.

3

Processes and Techniques

Any artistic activity requires a series of techniques, which are directly related to a procedure and to a method that makes its execution possible. We will revisit this in the step-by-step exercises. At this point, before we begin making small objects, we will look at how the tools and materials are used. In previous chapters, we described the materials, the tools, and the small implements from a theoretical perspective; now, we will explain their practical use. Sometimes, the techniques involved in using these tools and materials are a matter of simple mechanical movements that are repeated periodically, but most of them provide the foundation with which to create, in the future, whatever we feel like making, practically without limits on the imagination.

Sewing

There are a variety of sewing techniques for binding; however, in this section we will mention only the simplest and most useful ones. They will be used to do the exercises that are explained later on.

There are different types of twine for sewing besides the natural thread of vegetable origin, line hemp, and linen, which have been used forever. Nylon is also a possibility, and because of its durability and affordability, it can be practical for sewing books.

Sewing Loose Sheets

It is important to pay attention to the margin of the book with this type of sewing because it will inevitably be reduced during the process. This type of sewing is solid, as long as the paper is in good condition; otherwise, the first and last pages will have to be reinforced.

1- Several loose pages that need to be sewn at the spine.

2- Organize the pages and place them in the proper order. Apply a thin layer of glue on the spine. Then, make holes vertically with an awl at about ⅛ inch (3 mm) from the inner margin.

3- Thread the crease from the bottom to the top beginning with the first hole, at which point you make a knot. From that point, always proceeding from bottom to top, continue passing the thread through all the holes in order until the end. At that point, make another knot as you did at the beginning.

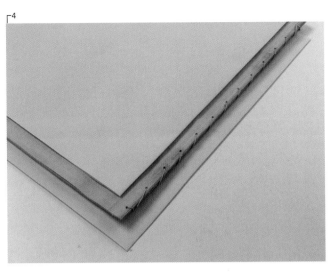

4- When the pastedowns are adhered, you should attempt to cover the sewn part completely.

Sewing a One-Page Signature

This type of sewing is very useful for any kind of pamphlet, regardless of the number of pages used. As in sewing loose sheets, the outside of the paper should be reinforced with paper or percale, if the paper is in poor condition.

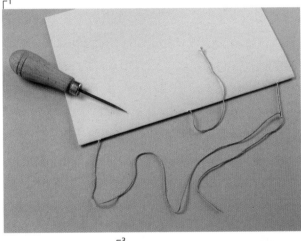

1- Since you will be sewing through the center of a single sheet, you only need to make three holes before you stitch it. One of them is made right in the middle, and the other two are made at ⅝ to ¾ inches (1.5 to 2 cm) from the head and tail. Insert the threaded needle in the middle hole from outside in and pull it out through one of the other holes, then insert it again through the hole at the other end.

2- The needle inside of the sheet will come out through the middle hole.

3- Tie a knot with the two loose ends of the cord, tying it around the long piece of thread that extends from one outside hole to the other.

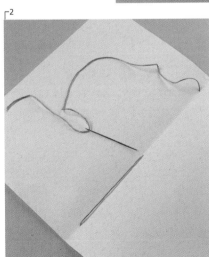

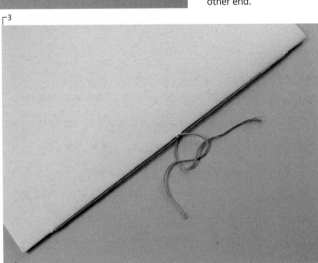

Sewing a Multiple-Page Signature

This is a simple type of sewing when multiple pages are involved. Sew with as many pages as you want, making the booklet easy to open when finished. Because the pages lay flat, this technique is used for pamphlets as well as for sheet music.

1- Take a few sheets and cut four equidistant holes with a saw, making sure that the two outer ones are approximately ⅜ to ⅝ inches (1 to 1.5 cm) from the top and the bottom.

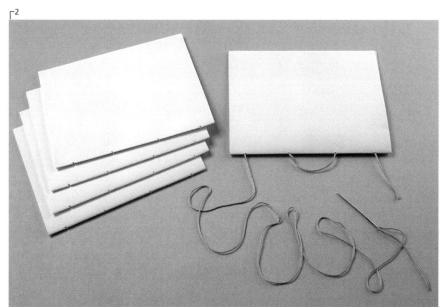

2- Insert the threaded needle through one of the outer holes on the first sheet pulling it from the outside. Pull it in and out through the three remaining holes the same way.

3- Take the second sheet and place it in the same direction as the previous one so the serrated notches line up; insert the threaded needle through the side hole and proceed as before. When you are finished, tie a couple of knots to secure it.

4- Repeat the same operation for the second sheet with the third one. When finished tie a chain knot with the previous sheet. Continue until the booklet is finished, at which point tie a double knot to make it stronger.

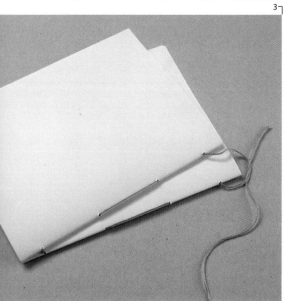

Exposed Sewing

Exposed sewing or a similar technique can be found in document bundles from the eighteenth century. This type of bonding is easy to open and does not require glue on the spine to finish it. The color threads and the different sewing patterns give it a modern look.

1- This technique can be done in many ways. In this case, begin, like before, by making four equidistant holes. Mark similar holes with an awl on a hard support, which will become the cover.

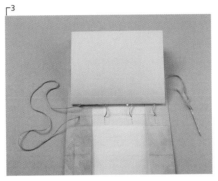

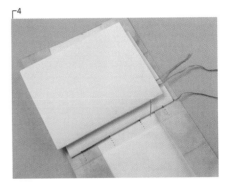

2- After making a loop through two of the holes on the first sheet, tie a knot with the thread to secure it.

3- As with the previous exercise, go in and out of the sheet with the needle, but this time go through the spine of the cover, where holes were previously made with an awl.

4- Insert the needle through the outside of the sheet to repeat the sewing process through the cover.

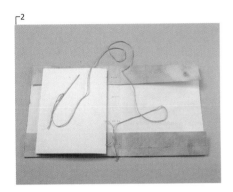

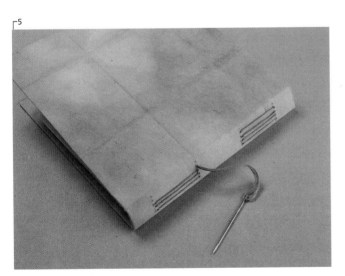

5- The stitching can be seen on the outside of the spine.

6- By sewing on the outside of the spine, the twine creates a decorative pattern that looks like a series of lines, which give the book an informal appearance. If you wanted to cover up the twine, then proceed as if you were sewing ribbons, which will be explained next.

Sewing with Ribbons

This is one of the variants that we mentioned before. Sewing with ribbons provides a stronger finish and keeps the sheets tighter together. Because the book, once sewn, can be opened completely flat, this method is also used for sheet music.

1- The sheets, once formed, are placed between two boards to be notched. Two of the holes will be located at ⅝ inches (1.5 cm) from the top and the bottom, while the others (at least four) will be in pairs, separated according to the ribbon's width. You will use more or fewer ribbons depending on the size of the booklet.

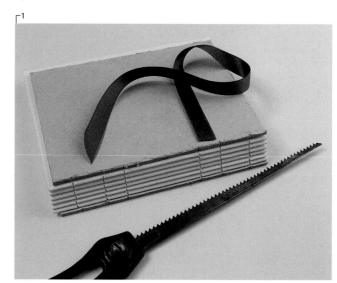

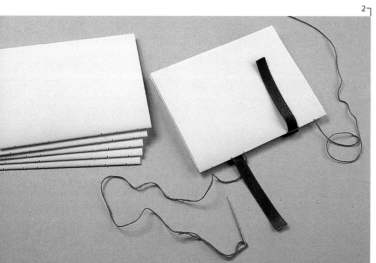

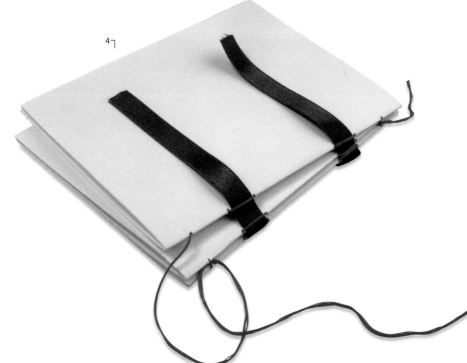

2- Insert the threaded needle from one of the ends and pull it out through the next hole to insert it once again, but this time hold the ribbon in place directly from the back. Continue to the end of the sheet, at which point you will pull the twine until there is no more than 2¾ to 3⅛ inches (7 or 8 cm) left hanging.

3- Repeat the same operation on the second sheet as with the first, tying the twine taut with the loose end.

4- Follow the same procedure with the third sheet and all the rest, remembering to tie a knot every time you finish one loop. When you finish the last sheet, make a double knot.

Japanese-Style Sewing

There are many ways of holding sheets of paper together. The Japanese style creates a visible sewing design; it is not a specific method or an unchangeable form of holding paper.

In this brief section, we will explain one of the many possible sewing patterns. Because of its simplicity and elegance, we think it deserves to be mentioned here.

1- With an awl, make a series of equidistant holes at ⅜ to ¾ inches (1 to 2 cm) from the spine. Use a ruler or a divider for this task because the holes must have the same distance between them.

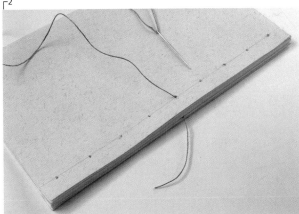

2- In this case, you will make nine holes along the spine. From the bottom, insert a threaded needle through the center hole and then pull it through. Then, insert the needle in the next hole and, once again, pull it through.

3- When the cord is taut, hold the spine firmly and bring the threaded needle around the spine so that you can insert it again into the same hole.

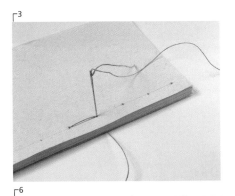

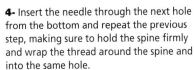

4- Insert the needle through the next hole from the bottom and repeat the previous step, making sure to hold the spine firmly and wrap the thread around the spine and into the same hole.

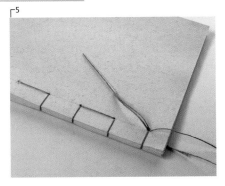

5- Repeat the previous operation as many times as there are holes, until you reach the last one, then sew the end part vertically and horizontally at the same time.

6- Following from top to bottom and bottom to top, cover the spaces where there is no cord, until you again reach the center of the booklet, where you started.

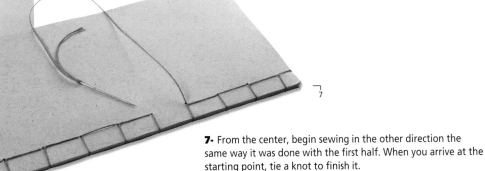

7- From the center, begin sewing in the other direction the same way it was done with the first half. When you arrive at the starting point, tie a knot to finish it.

Gluing

This is an important section within the chapter on processes and techniques, since, in addition to the conventional adhesives that are sold in specialized stores, there are other types of adhesives that you can make for use with the various materials and surfaces. Sometimes, when more than one type of glue can be used for a job, you may choose a specific one just because it is clean and easy to use.

Making Adhesive Paste

Paste is perhaps the most common adhesive for gluing paper. It has been used by artists for a long time, and it is usually made by hand by the bookbinder, even though many with similar characteristics are available on the market. This product takes a long time to dry, it makes the paper buckle, and it crystallizes when it dries. To begin, pour three parts water and one part flour into a pot. Break up the flour with your fingers to prevent it from forming lumps and then set the pot on the stove. Stir it with a brush continuously and somewhat vigorously to prevent it from burning.

When the water begins to boil, remove the pot from the stove and let the mixture cool off. At that point, it will be ready for use. Some chemical products could prevent the paste from breaking down easily; however, it is best to make only the amount needed. It can be stored in the refrigerator for a few days and still maintain all its properties.

Finished paste.

Materials required for the preparation of the paste.

How to Prepare the Mixture

As the title indicates, this glue is a mixture of polyvinyl acetate, better known as bookbinding plastic glue, and tilosa, or wallpaper glue.

First, mix tilosa in water and let it rest until it is completely diluted. It must remain thick, to the point of showing resistance when spreading it with a brush. Once the tilosa and water are ready, add the plastic glue to the contents; even though the proportions are not too important, it would be advisable to use two parts wallpaper glue to one of plastic glue. You can use a brush or a small blender to mix it and add a small amount of water until it has the desired consistency when dissolved. To check the mixture, dip a brush into the mixture and pull it out to observe if a drop drips from it slowly. This glue is very easy to work

Plastic glue and tilosa are used to prepare the mixture.

Consistency that must be achieved (the drop is being formed little by little).

with and has a slower drying time than plastic glue. It works especially well when used to adhere large surfaces.

Rubber Cement

Rubber cement is perhaps the least used adhesive. It is good for adhering nonporous surfaces, like plastic, metal, small pieces of glass, and other elements. The glue is applied to both surfaces. If the surface in question is quite large, the glue can be spread with a spatula (a piece of cardboard can also be used instead).

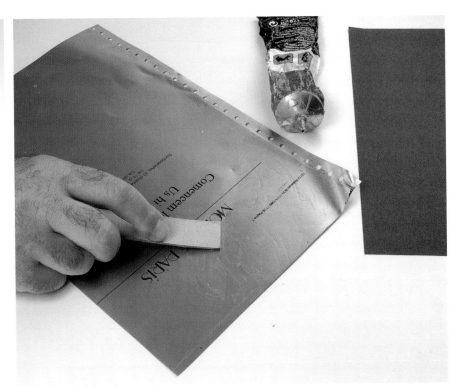

A piece of cardboard can serve as a spatula to spread rubber cement over the surface.

The Paper Fibers

All papers have different types of fibers; these tend to be elongated and aligned in the same direction. Japanese paper and some other handmade papers are exceptions. The direction of the fiber is very important in the bookbinding process.

The lines drawn on the paper indicate the direction of the fiber. The cardboard is more flexible in this direction than in the opposite one because the fibers are elongated.

1- To understand the importance of the fiber's direction in bookbinding we are going to conduct a simple experiment. We will use two sheets of paper of the same type, size and weight, one of them cut with the grain and the other cut against the grain.

2- The fibers of the paper on the left go in widthwise, while those on the right go lengthwise. We cover both with a thin layer of paste to soften them.

3- Notice how both curl differently. When the paper's fibers, which are elongated, get wet, they have a tendency to swell up. This is why the paper grows in the opposite direction of the fibers; the width increases, but the length does not. In every binding process, we will be counteracting the stretching effect of the paper to achieve the effective drying and proper finish of the piece.

The direction of the fibers in any fabric or paper that is rolled up is always parallel to the edges of the roll. That is why it tears easily in this direction but with difficulty in the opposite one. Toilet tissue has a perforated line across it to facilitate tearing.

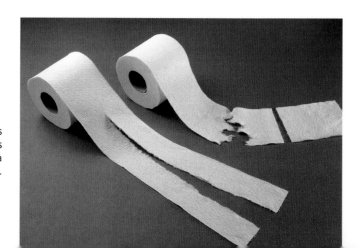

Preparing Ordinary Fabric

For many reasons, you may sometimes want to use a piece of cloth to line an object. The ideal in this case is for it to have some degree of consistency so the glue does not seep through; however, there are methods to improve thinner fabrics for this use.

1- Select the fabric you want to use. If you apply glue directly to the fabric with a brush, the glue will most probably seep through and stain its good side. To prevent this from happening, apply a thin layer of glue to a piece of paper the same size as the fabric.

2- Adhere the fabric to the paper and leave it to dry under a heavy weight (not under a press). If the fabric is very thin, you will need to apply a backing to it with an iron and then adhere it to the paper.

Follow the same procedure for Japanese or light and very porous papers; this will give them greater consistency and make them easier to handle.

Gluing the Pastedowns, Headbands, and Spine

Since this is an operation that without a doubt is going to be repeated each time a book is bound, it is a good idea to understand the concepts very well.

Cleanliness and order are paramount in this process; otherwise, the pages of the book could get stained.

1- To attach the pastedowns onto the first and last pages of a book, stagger them placing one sheet over the other and then apply the glue with a brush. This way, the glue will be evenly distributed over the entire surface.

2- When the pastedowns are in place, make a headband with the same color. To do this, you need a piece of paper and a length of twine.

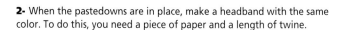

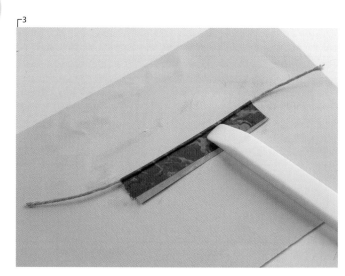

3- Glue the paper and then place the twine in its center. When the paper is folded over, you are left with the thickness of the twine, which will be pressed in place with the bone folder. Leave it out to dry.

4- Apply glue to the spine and attach the headbands on the top and the bottom, letting them extend over on both sides. Place the lining between the two headbands, trying not to overlap.

When it dries, make the headbands conform to the size of the book.

Double Layering

Double layering is a very useful technique to give a specific object more consistency, whether it is a box or book covers.

Begin with the concept that two pieces of cardboard of a specific thickness glued together have greater strength than a single one twice the thickness.

When the dimensions require it, you will need to double layer the boards. This consists of gluing the boards together so they can be thicker and stronger. Keep in mind though that a very thick board cannot be cut with the sheer.

Inserting a Ribbon

Sometimes a ribbon will need to be inserted into the board when making a folder, a box, or a similar object.

This simple operation is often disregarded because it is so easy; but it is important to remember that a poorly placed ribbon can ruin the overall appearance of the piece.

Make a hole with a craft knife or chisel on the board exactly where the ribbon is going to be inserted. The ribbon is inserted from the outside with the help of a bone folder and then glued in place. Tap it with a hammer when it is dry to flatten it out.

Sometimes, depending on the function of the ribbon, as in the case illustrated here, a punch will be needed to make a round and clean opening to insert the ribbon folded. Once the ribbon comes out it can be unfolded.

Cuts and Folds

This section deserves special attention within the chapter on processes and techniques.

During the binding process, the pieces will have a variety of forms and shapes and they may require different types of cuts and folds. Here, there are a variety of objects to illustrate these finishes. The tools that are normally used are also studied, as are the types of adhesive that can be used in each case.

Cutting Paper and Boards

Based on the work being done, cuts and folds are the first thing that comes to mind. Specific machines and tools are needed to carry them out and to achieve the appropriate finish in each case.

The guillotine can cut through considerable thicknesses, and the sheer is good for individual boards and sheets of paper. Sometimes, for whatever reason, the sheets are cut by signature with the sheer, while the covers, that is, the board, will be cut with the guillotine.

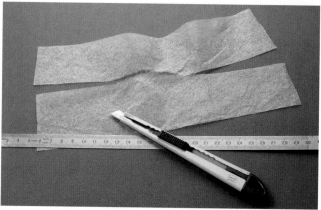

The craft knife or cutter is a basic tool for cutting paper and board; however, when very thin Japanese paper with long fibers has to be cut, this tool can tear it rather than cut it, ruining the paper.

The scalpel, due to the curved shape of its incision, can be used to cut paper that has long fibers into thin strips.

Folding and Finishing Borders

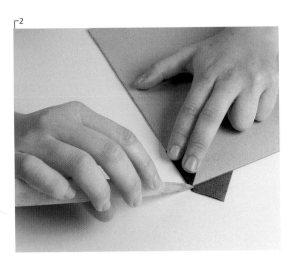

There are many ways of finishing the ends of a book cover as well as a mathematical proportion for folding the corners of a cover into points. Let's look at some examples here.

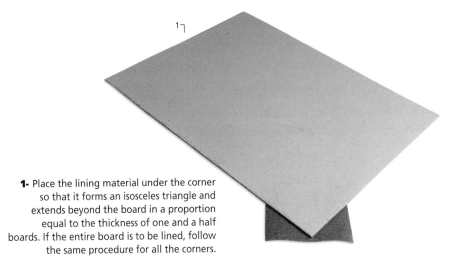

1- Place the lining material under the corner so that it forms an isosceles triangle and extends beyond the board in a proportion equal to the thickness of one and a half boards. If the entire board is to be lined, follow the same procedure for all the corners.

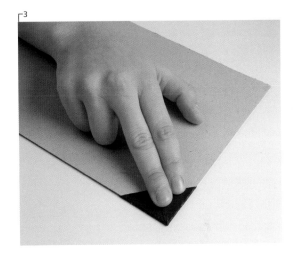

2- After one of the sides has been folded over, tuck the small tip in with the help of a finger or a bone folder.

3- The corner is finished after the second side is folded over the first one.

1- This is another way of folding a corner; there is no cutting involved. It is used with lightweight papers and fabrics because thicker paper when folded may cause an ugly lump that can ruin the overall appearance.

2- Once the corner of the paper or fabric has been folded inward forming an isosceles triangle, fold over one of its sides.

3- Fold over the second side the same way, and the edge will have been finished in a way that looks different and elegant.

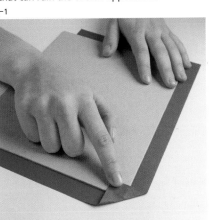

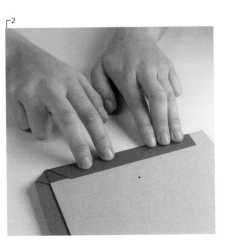

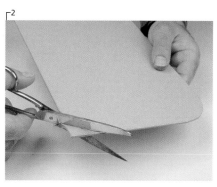

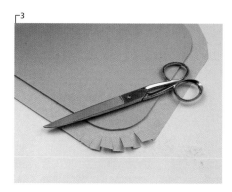

1- Sometimes you may need to make round corners; for this, you can use the compass or a round object, or in this case the lid of a jar.

2- Give it the desired shape with scissors. If the board is very thick you may have to file the edge of the curve with sandpaper mounted on a piece of wood, which will make it easier to handle.

3- With scissors or a craft knife, make small cuts on the fabric, following the curvature of the board and trying not to cut all the way to the edge.

4- Fold the fabric over the board carefully, trying to overlap the small cut out pieces one over the other in an orderly fashion.

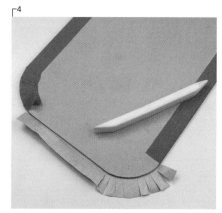

5- Even out the edge with the bone folder. This should be done before the glue has dried out completely.

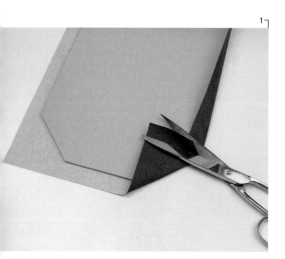

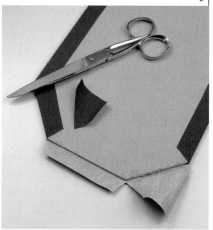

1- Another frequent fold is one that is irregular in shape. To make it, fold the fabric over the corner forming a pleat and then make a cut with the scissors as shown in the picture.

2- When the fold is complete, you will notice that the excess paper has to be trimmed to make all the edges the same.

3- Adjust and tighten all the corners and the angles trying to avoid the formation of air pockets in the fabric.

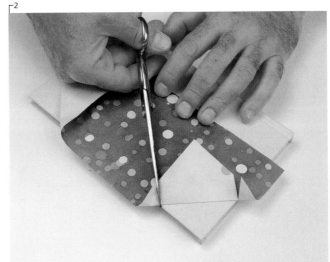

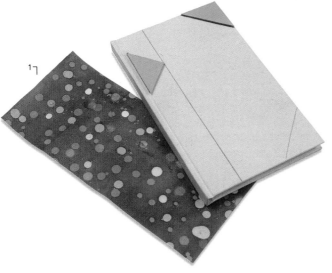

1- For the final example of a corner fold, we present the one used for lining a booklet. In this case, the area of the part that touches the spine will be smaller than one third of the size of the cover and the height of the triangle that forms the corner will have the same dimension. With a pencil, mark the outlines on the cover.

2- Place the paper where marked, covering the pencil lines; then fold the corners inward leaving the tips of the book uncovered. With scissors, make a cut perpendicular to this fold, directly in the area that borders with the cover.

3- Make a cut with a craft knife to remove the excess paper. To make sure that the lining fits within the designated space, it is helpful to mark with a pencil the upper and lower areas of the paper opposite the corners.

4- In this view of the paper lining the cover, you can see that the spine and the corners have a balanced proportion.

5- In this view of the corners from the inside, notice how the fold creates the same angle inside as it does outside.

Cuts and Folds in a Box

Many boxes can be recycled and reused or be given a particular look by lining them with paper.

1- For this exercise we will use an old pencil holder that is worn from use.

2- Here, there are paper and glue. The paper will be somewhat longer than the perimeter of the pencil holder, while the width will be the same as its height plus ⅝ inch (1.5 cm) on each side.

3- Place the box in the center of the paper, making sure that the distance from the top and the bottom is the same. Since the box is small, the single piece of paper will wrap all around it. Be mindful of the joint formed by the two ends, making sure that it falls on one of the corners of the box so the piece is esthetically pleasing.

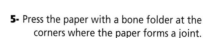

4- Cut the part of the paper that is folded to the inside with scissors, beginning at the bottom and going all the way to the end of the paper against the corner. This will be a very delicate cut to make sure that as little paper as possible is removed so it can cover the inside edge when the paper is folded over.

5- Press the paper with a bone folder at the corners where the paper forms a joint.

6- Unlike the cuts made on the upper part, the cuts at the bottom will begin at the corners and will remove as much paper as possible to avoid unnecessary thicknesses.

7- After reinforcing the sides, you will only need to add a base to the bottom area and the piece will be finished.

Compartments in a Tray

How many times have you thought about creating compartments in a drawer or a box to store small pieces to prevent them from mixing together? Here is a simple way to do it.

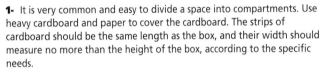

1- It is very common and easy to divide a space into compartments. Use heavy cardboard and paper to cover the cardboard. The strips of cardboard should be the same length as the box, and their width should measure no more than the height of the box, according to the specific needs.

2- This is how the cardboard pieces are lined, removing excess paper from the ends with scissors.

3- With a craft knife, make a few cuts all along the board so they can be linked together. The cuts will go slightly beyond the halfway mark in width and have approximately the same thickness as the cardboard.

4- View of the partitions finished and put in place.

Two Types of Lids

Cardboard trays can have different uses, but they would be much more practical if they had lids. In this brief section we will demonstrate the construction of two different lids: one attached to the base and the other unattached.

Attached Lid

This lid is attached to the base, forming half the box. It is a very simple cover.

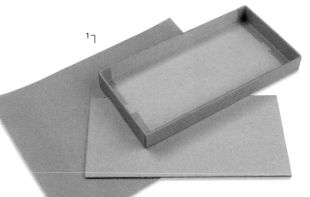

1- Cover and line three of the four sides of a tray. Cut a piece of cardboard the same size as the base, which will become the lid.

2- With the paper placed as shown, line the board that will become the lid, folding all the sides over except the side that will be connected to the base. Notice that the paper, when folded, is forced in such way that the loose end is somewhat narrower than the board.

3- Center the board of the lid over the box and place a ruler at the edge that is to be folded, to allow some space between the two pieces. Once the paper is glued, fold it over the spine and the lower part.

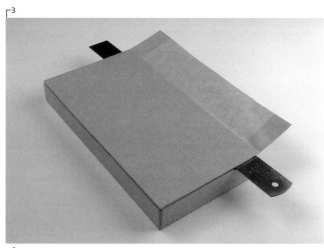

4- With a piece of paper that fits the back of the lid and a small amount of glue, line the lid plus the side of the box and ⅜ inch (1 cm) of the base. Because of the space that was left between the two cardboard pieces with the ruler, it is possible to carry out this operation without forcing the paper, allowing the fit in the area of the hinge not to obstruct the closing of the lid.

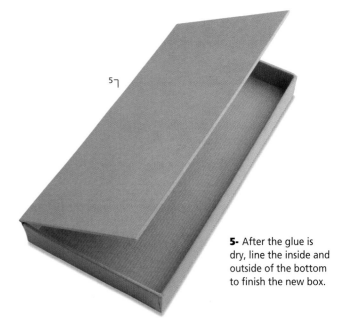

5- After the glue is dry, line the inside and outside of the bottom to finish the new box.

Detached Lid

As in the previous exercise we select a tray that is lined as needed, reserving part of the matching paper to make a hard lid.

In this case, it is a very nice and elegant lid.

1- To make the lid, cut two pieces of board that is somewhat heavy; one will be exactly the size of the outside of the tray, while the second one will be the same size as the base measured from the inside of the box, that is, leaving out the thickness of the side boards.

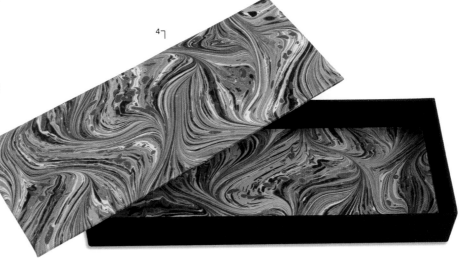

2- The two board pieces that will become the lid are lined separately, according to the colors established beforehand.

3- Adhere the two resulting pieces with thick glue; then center the smaller one over the larger one, leaving the same edge on all four sides. When this is finished, put them aside under a weight to let them dry completely and to prevent any buckling.

4- The lid, once finished, must fit perfectly over the base, turning this into a practical yet decorative object.

Scoring

Many times we need to score a board or piece of paper. Although this is usually easy, it can be a delicate procedure due to its simplicity. Besides, in some exercises and objects, scoring may be the one and only procedure involved, as in the case of the two examples shown here: the accordion and the cardboard book box.

Accordion

The accordion model has become a classic in the world of crafts; it is useful for storing photos, papers, clippings, and more.

1- To make an accordion, prepare strips of cardboard of a desired width. A cardboard template will help define the location of the folds. On a piece of white construction paper, mark these folds by scoring them with a bone folder.

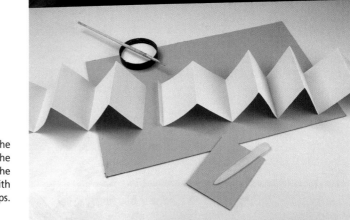

2- To ensure that all the folds are the same, it is important to turn the template over at every score. If there is a small difference in the placement of the template, it will become more noticeable each time the bone folder is marked. If this occurs, the pages will not fold evenly. With a touch of glue, adhere the completed strips.

3- When the pieces are folded, cut out two board panels that measure approximately ⅛ inch (3 mm) more on each side than the construction paper. Line the boards and let them dry.

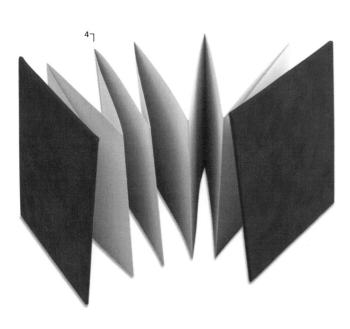

4- Glue the lined pieces to the front and back of the accordion. When completed it can be used for storing photos, writings, or mementos of various thicknesses since this piece has no spine. When it is filled, it can be stored inside a box.

Cardboard Case for Books

Many times we want to protect a book, either to avoid damaging the quality material of its covers, or simply to make it unique.

This solution, based on origami, or the art of folding paper, makes it possible to complete this project with a single piece of construction paper.

1- Take a piece of construction paper that has the width of the book's height, and a height of four times the width of the book plus its own thickness.
Score lines marking the thickness of the book in the center as well as on the upper and lower parts. Also, score the areas beyond the spine that will measure the same as the panel of the book.

2- With a craft knife, make a cut in the scoring of the head and tail areas. This will go up to the middle of the right and left panels, respectively. Then, fold them in.

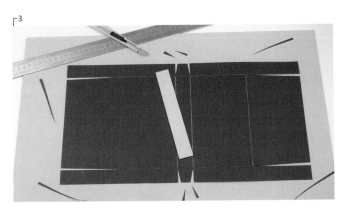

3- Cut the construction paper to make sure that it will not overlap when folded. Also cut a piece of paper for the area of the spine, which will measure ½₄ inch (1 mm) less in width and height.

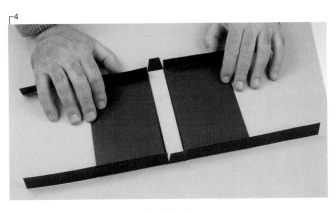

4- When the piece of paper is glued on the center, fold the piece according to the scoring previously marked.

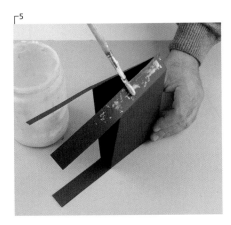

5- With a brush and thick glue, adhere the upper and lower flaps together.

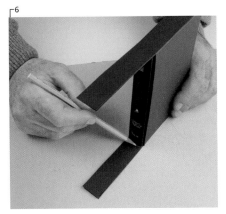

6- When the cover is dry, insert the book in it, leaving the rounded part of the spine out. Mark the head and tail parts with a pencil, exactly where the excess board should be cut.

7- This way the book is protected and individualized.

Projects and Decoration

This is an important part of the book because, in addition to the exercises mentioned so far, there are many other projects that can be created. To make them, it is important to be familiar with the trade and, especially, to be creative and to enjoy the process. In this brief section, we will introduce some examples that we hope will serve as a springboard for the creation of many other projects.

How to Make a Cushioned Surface

The covers for books, booklets, photo albums, and a variety of other objects can be cushioned inside. Their finish is elegant, but its execution very easy.

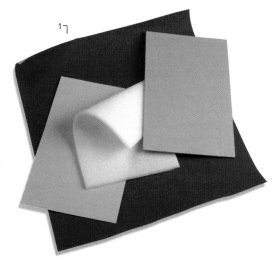

1- Take a piece of foam about ⅛ inch (3 or 4 mm) thick, a heavy cardboard, construction paper, and the material we will use for lining.

2- Cut the construction paper, the foam, and the heavy board all the same size and layer them in this order. At the same time cut the fabric somewhat larger so it can be folded over on the back.

3- When the fabric is folded and glued over the thick board, incorporate the construction paper, pressing the foam and creating the desired cushioned effect.

How to Paint the Ends of Books

It is preferable to paint the ends of a book before mounting the covers; however, if the book is already bound and you want to protect it from the dust, you can still paint the ends as long as you take the necessary precautions.

1- Place the book with the covers completely open. Protecting the ends between two pieces of cardboard, place the book at the edge of a wood board, and then paint the ends with a brush and aniline dyes dissolved in water.

2- Once dry, rub the ends with a cotton ball and then apply wax.

Several Cover Samples

Let's say that we want to construct a book cover that contains a window, to frame something inside of it.

1- There are several papers of different weights and colors where one of the edges has been burned. Make a pleasing arrangement with the papers, which have been previously varnished to prevent them from getting dirty, to make the cover with a piece of cardboard as a base.

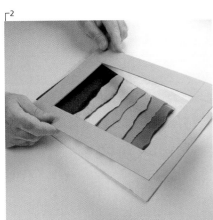

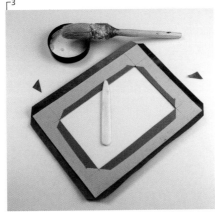

2- Position a cardboard frame cut to size that fits over the prepared base.

3- Line the frame folding over only the inside part.

4- Once the glue is dry, attach the frame to the base where the papers are arranged, and fold the sides around the base. When this is complete, the composition is finished.

Window to Hold a Picture

This is the solution needed when we want to place a picture or a flat object inside a cover to protect it from the usual wear and tear from pulling it in and out of the shelf.

1- The objective is to decorate the cover of a book with an illustration from a newspaper or magazine. Lacquer is needed to varnish the illustration as well as the material needed to make the covers: boards of three different thicknesses, a piece of construction paper, fabric to line it, and board for the spine.

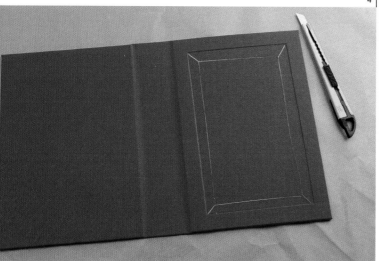

2- When the board for the cover has been cut to size, mark the mid-size board where the opening is located, apply glue to it, and place it exactly over the construction paper. Then press it and let it dry.

3- With a ruler and a craft knife, make a window in the construction paper, leaving the initial base with a frame around it.

4- When the lid is mounted, and before it dries, make a few cuts in the fabric at approximately ⅜ inch (1 cm) from the frame and adjust it with the bone folder. This way, the fabric is completely adhered to the frame.

5- In the resulting space, glue the selected cut out piece, which has been lacquered beforehand.

1- The same procedure can be used for different shapes and elements.

2- The thickness of the board that holds the pieces protects them from potential wear and tear.

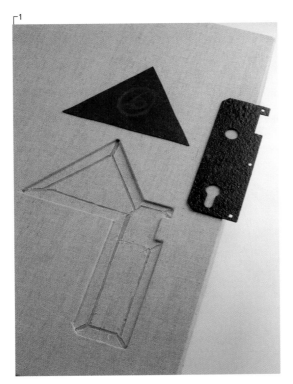

1- Here is another way to create the depression on the cover when it is small. Take the paper that is to be glued inside the space and thick boards of the same dimensions as the paper.

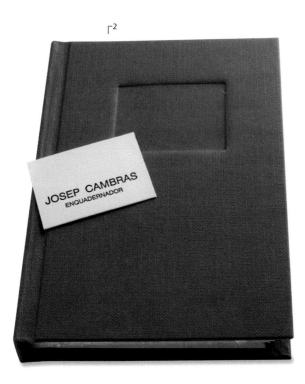

2- Place the piece where chosen and apply great amounts of pressure with the press to create the depression. To achieve a proper finish, this operation must be carried out on the detached cover or with the book wide open.

Texture with Newspapers

Use your imagination to construct your own textures and forms to make the covers of a book. Here is one example of the many possible alternatives using newspaper as a base.

1- The first step is to soften the paper, which can be done by coating it with several layers of very diluted paste.

2- Place the softened paper on a paper support, either crumpling it, spreading it, or tearing it up. It remains adhered to the paper due to the adhesive paste.

3- Once the paper has been distributed while trying not to create too many lumps, flatten it out with the palms of your hands. A sheet of plastic can be helpful in this procedure since it is a non-porous material.

4- When it is completely dry, paint it. In this case, we chose gold spray paint.

5- To prepare the cover where the textured paper is to be glued, place two cardboard pieces to create a riser so the surface will be completely leveled.

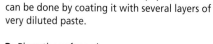

6- Once the cardboard pieces have been properly placed, they are lined, making sure to cover the resulting small edge with the help of the bone folder.

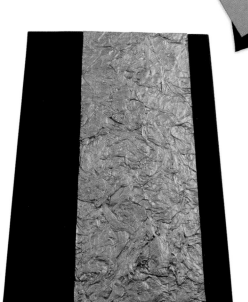

7- View of the finished textured paper.

Paper Cutouts

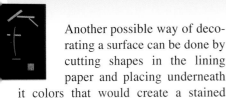

Another possible way of decorating a surface can be done by cutting shapes in the lining paper and placing underneath it colors that would create a stained glass effect.

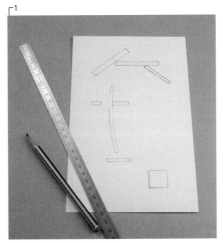

1- To carry out this decoration, sketch the design that you want to achieve. This pattern cannot be improvised and does not allow for corrections.

2- Using the sketch, or a photocopy of it as a reference, cut out the designs that will decorate the cover.

3- Once the pieces have been cut out, choose the papers that will be used in the design. Glue the color papers to the back of the lining paper. This is done with very thick and sparsely applied glue, or with an adhesive spray, to keep the paper that will line the cover from buckling.

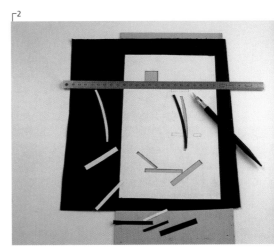

4- When the glue has dried, the lining paper can be adhered to the cover board. To achieve a good finish, you must keep in mind the thickness of the color papers as well as the glue application to prevent their thickness from being noticeable on the front.

Decorating with Juxtaposed Papers

As the name itself indicates, this decorative motif is created with papers of different weights, textures, and colors, composing geometric shapes that include a variety of colored square and rectangular figures.

The papers should not overlap, but should be glued juxtaposed to each other, that is, glued together side by side.

Simple Restorations

We hope that this section will be very useful for fixing the books that are showing some wear and tear or that may hold memories of old family members who are part of our lives. This method will try to improve their condition while maintaining their original appearance as much as possible.

To do this, you can use the products that can be found around the house, without getting too deep into the restoration world, which would require another chapter.

Reconstructing the Spine

Here is a book that is in one piece but has lost a large part of its spine and suffered damage on the surfaces of both its covers. To repair the book without dismantling it, you can construct a new spine preserving the area that contains the title.

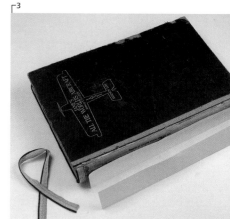

1- This book has suffered some damage on the spine and shows some wear and tear on its covers, but it is in sound condition inside: the sewing is good and the pastedowns are solid.

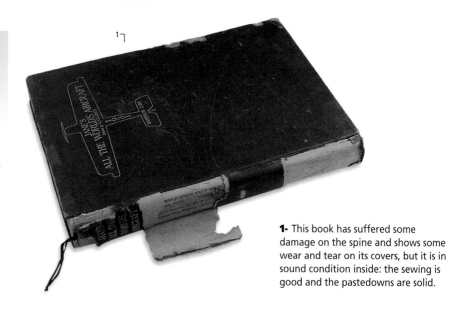

2- Remove the parts of the spine that are still there and save them. Using a craft knife and a ruler remove the cloth from the spine, as well as approximately ⅜ inch (1 cm) from the cover along both sides of the spine.

3- Once the spine is clean, prepare the headband and the paper that will become the hollow. This is a paper folded in thirds that should be as wide as the spine and that will form a hollow area when the two exterior flaps are glued on.

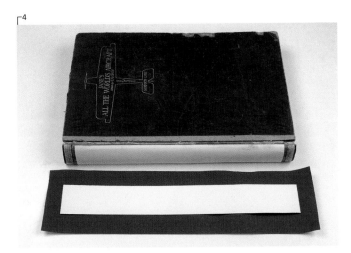

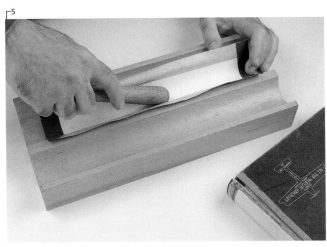

4- After gluing the hollow and the headbands, as shown in the picture, cut what will be the new spine. This will be as long as the covers and as wide as the book's spine. At the same time, also cut the cloth that will line the spine. This will have the same dimensions as the spine plus ⅝ to ¾ inches (1.5 to 2 cm) on each side.

5- Glue the board on the cloth perfectly centered and fold the cloth over the board only in the areas of the head and the tail. When it dries it is shaped in the spine rounding form.

6- Glue the book's spine and the cloth's flaps. Keep it centered on the book and glued to it. Before it dries, cut the excess cloth from the front and back with a craft knife and a ruler.

7- Since the cloth is not dry it is easily dislodged, leaving it at the same level as the original book.

8- The part of the spine that will be preserved is adhered to Japanese paper and left to dry before cutting.

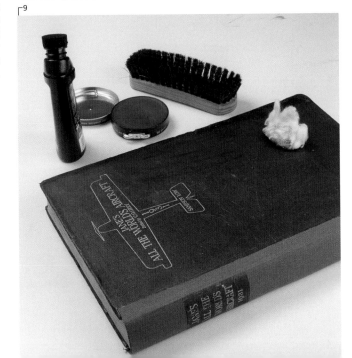

9- Once the part of the original, preserved spine is cut to the desired size, it is glued onto the new spine. Touch up the areas where material is missing with shoe polish, markers, paints, and so on. Finally, seal the colors so they do not stain the adjacent books.

Loose Covers and End Papers

This is another common problem in a worn book. It involves a small book that only has the spine intact and the leather covers; the end papers have become detached as a result of wear and tear.

1- Due to usage, the exterior leather that protects the book is no longer attached, but the spine is. The pastedowns as well as the first and last pages attached to the covers are also loose.

2- Since the book is small and therefore light, you can employ a simple solution that will keep it together and that will make it strong and usable so it can be handled again. Remove the spine from the book carefully with a scalpel to avoid any damage.

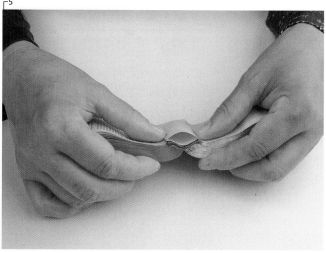

3- With a piece of paper and a pencil, measure the spine to make the hollow.

4- When the hollow has been measured, form the classic triptych making the ends of the exterior flats meet, and glue it to the book's covers.

5- Once glued and dried, notice the presence of the hollow when you open the book, which will protect the spine when it returns to its place.

6- Make sure that the pastedowns and the end papers are in good condition. Then, attach them with a thin layer of glue.

7- The book and the covers will form a unit. Attach a piece of Japanese paper to the backside of the spine, which is still detached, leaving excess paper on all four sides. Let it dry.

8- Once dry, glue the spine over the entire hollow leaving the excess Japanese paper in place.

9- Using tilosa, glue the Japanese paper onto the cover, removing the excess paper. Once dry, cut a small strip of paper and glue it where the surfaces and the spine meet to protect the spine on its front.

10- If the head and tail of the book were in poor condition, you could add a small piece of paper to strengthen them. Once dry, apply a thin layer of tilosa over the entire surface, which in addition to adhering the Japanese paper will seal the damaged leather.

4 Paper Painting Techniques

With just these six different methods or approaches for painting paper, you should not expect to become an expert on the subject, since for that one needs to practice with the materials constantly to get to know them well. The density of the water and the dyes, as well as the consistency and porosity of the paper make each project an adventure.

Painting Paper

The creativity in terms of the drawings, their designs, and the way the colors are combined make this chapter a clear example of the many possibilities available.

With this approach, you can use the papers to later construct the objects that you want, giving a different personality and charisma to each one of them.

How to Paint Paper with Repeated Motifs

This classic technique, which was used in Italy during the Renaissance, can provide a great variety of designs and shapes. Even though it may appear simple, using repeated motifs can become complicated if we try to match colors and shapes.

Different materials can also be used. At the beginning, a piece of wood was used, although it is preferable to employ softer materials such as linoleum, erasers, or just a simple potato.

1- Cut a potato in two, which will give you two surfaces to carve out the desired design. To do this, use a cutting tool that will allow to make turns easily; it should be narrow and easy to handle.

2- The design possibilities are endless. You can choose several according to the effects that you want to create.

3- Dip the potato into the gouache as if it were an inking pad and stamp the design. If two or more colors and two or more designs are used, then proceed with care to make sure that they are combined as planned.

4- Here the paper is finished. By changing the background or the color of the ink, you will obtain completely different papers that can produce surprising effects.

You can also use a design carved on an eraser to repeat a single motif, like the one of the barbwire fence shown in this picture.

Other vegetables can also be used as stamps.

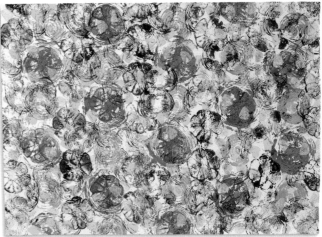

Sample of a paper with different colors and designs.

Marbleized Paper

Marbleizing is perhaps the painting technique that provides the most surprising results, as well as the best-known type of paper. Its origins can be traced to Turkey where it is called *ebru*. Elaborate shapes and designs, like flowers and animals, and a variety of other decorative motifs can be created with the procedure that we are going to explain here. To make the design, two important factors have to be taken into consideration: the density of the ink and the density of the water.

1- Pour ordinary wallpaper glue into water to give it a somewhat thick consistency.

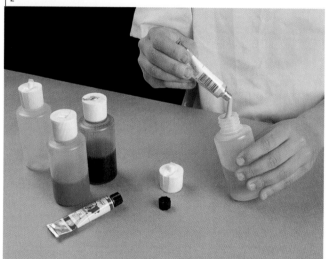

2- While the glue is dissolving in the water, begin to prepare the colors, which are oil paints mixed with gasoline. Pour the paint into the bottles filled with gasoline and shake them.

3- When the paints are poured into the pan, they float due to the density of the water. If the paint does not spread after being poured, but forms drops that do not dilute, then you must add more gasoline to the bottle.

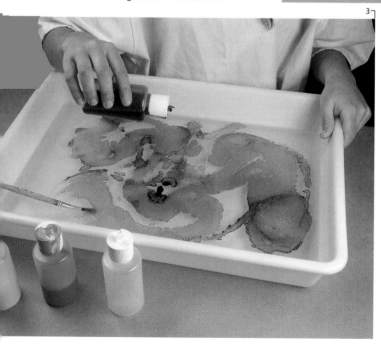
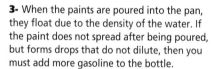

4- Repeat this step as many times as needed. Notice how the colors do not blend to form a third color, instead they spread around each other.

5- With a brush, a wooden stick, or a similar object, draw the designs in the water, stretching or compressing the colors as needed. In this case, we have created a classic pattern.

6- Hold the sides of the paper with both hands and lay it in the pan middle first, followed by the sides, which you will ease in carefully.

7- Wait until the paper settles in the water to prevent air bubbles from forming. Air bubbles could cause areas of unpainted paper in the midst of the colors.

8- Holding the paper at both ends, slide it over the edge of the pan. This causes the excess paint to drip off the painted paper.

9- View of the first paper sample.

Painting Paper with Wax

To paint paper with wax, you must have acrylic paints and a wax or paraffin candle. This is another variation of painted paper that can also be very pleasing, due to the unexpected results, which can be mastered only after a little practice.

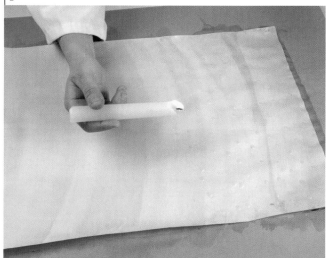

1- Prepare several containers of acrylic paint diluted in water. With a brush, apply a thick layer of paint, which will become the background of the paper.

2- With a lit candle, begin to apply drops of wax on the paper, which will create a reserve for the next layer of paint.

3- Apply a second layer of paint on the paper, over the drops of wax already dried, with a different color.

4- Once again, spread drops of wax over the paint.

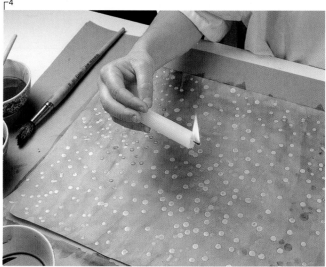

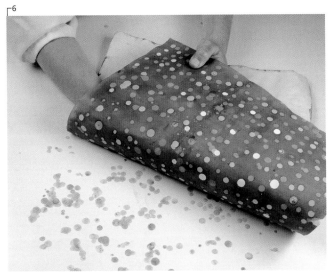

5- Paint is applied again. You can repeat this operation with the wax and the paint as many times as needed.

6- When you roll the paper, the drops of dry wax come off, leaving the reserves exposed.

7- Finished paper. If by any chance there are still drops of wax attached to the paper, this is the time to remove them with your fingers or with a scraper.

In this paper, we can see horizontal lines. These were made by drawing on the paper with the wax candle to make a reserve. A variety of effects can be achieved this way.

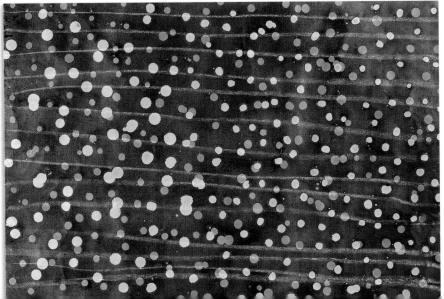
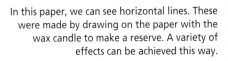

Crumpled Paper and Salt Paper

These are two simple techniques for painting paper that may be combined or not, as needed. It is a good paper for backgrounds, for end papers, booklets, and the like.

Not much experience is needed to create them, and spontaneity is an important part of the final result.

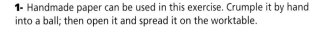

1- Handmade paper can be used in this exercise. Crumple it by hand into a ball; then open it and spread it on the worktable.

2- Wet the sponge in a dish containing gouache paint diluted in water and apply it all over the paper. The areas of the paper that have wrinkles will hold more water than the rest, creating an evenly distributed marbleized effect over the entire surface.

When the first layer is dry, a second layer of the same color or a brighter one will reinforce the desired effect.

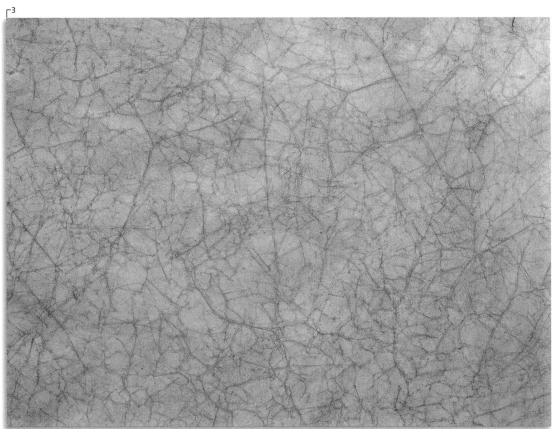

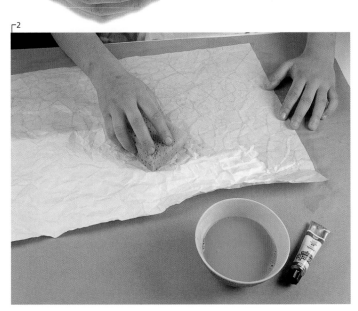

3- After leaving it under weights to dry, the paper is finished.

1- Next, you will work on a second paper that can be combined with the previous one. For this you need blotting or watercolor paper, gouache paints, and coarse salt. After diluting the paint, we proceed by applying it on the paper with a sponge per the crumpled paper technique. The layer of paint must be generous so the paper is completely soaked with the liquid that was just applied.

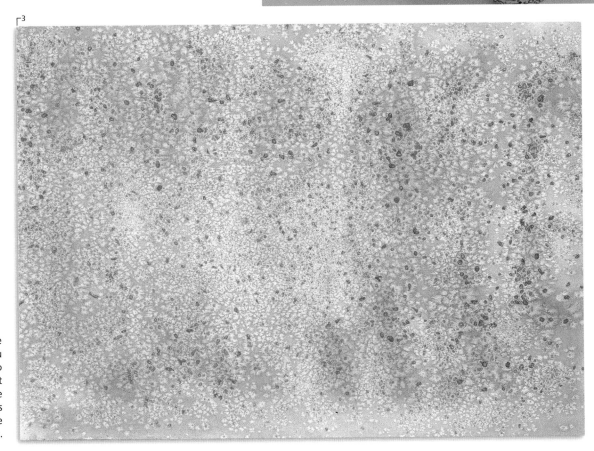

2- Before the paper dries out, sprinkle coarse salt over the entire surface. This makes the paint concentrate in the areas covered with the salt due to absorption.

3- When the paper is dry, you only need to remove the salt to achieve the result that is shown in the picture.

Paper Painted with Paste

Great painted-paper artists have practiced this technique widely with spectacular results. To do this, one needs a sense of composition and good knowledge of colors. However, attractive results can be achieved easily and simply without complete mastery of both requirements.

1- Place the glue paste in a container and add gouache paint for color.

2- Mix it with a brush until a uniform paste is created where the color is completely diluted.

3- Spread the colored paste on the paper. Even though in this particular case we are working with a single color, you can apply as many colors as needed to create the desired composition.

4- Now spend a few minutes working with the color. You can use any object, as well as your fingers, to make the desired designs and texture.

5- This monochromatic background has been created simply by using a hairbrush.

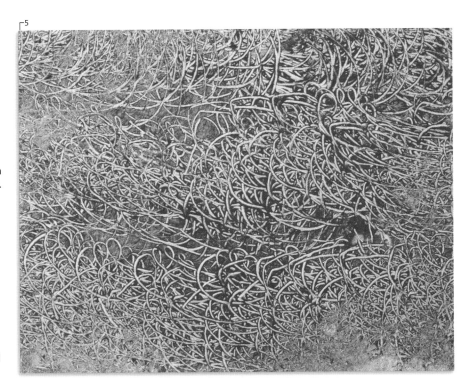

1- Using a spatula or a piece of cardboard is one of the many ways that paint can be spread on the paper.

2- With a small strip of cardboard, create different shapes such as lines and curves, as long as the paint is not completely dry.

3- Composition with a single color over color paper.

Painting Paper by Folding

For this type of design you will need gouache paint and Japanese paper, which is light and very porous. This is why you need to add strength to the paper when it is finished, which is done by gluing a heavier paper to one of its sides.

1- Take Japanese paper of some consistency and fold it to form different geometric figures.

2- You should have different containers of gouache that has been diluted in water. Insert one of the ends of the folded paper into one of the dishes. The porosity of the paper makes it act like blotting paper, absorbing the paint. Therefore, be careful not to keep it inside the liquid for a long time.

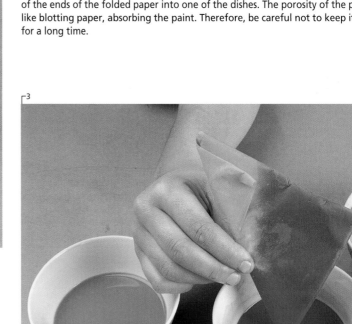

3- Repeat the previous operation by submerging the other tips of the paper into the different paints that we have prepared.

4- The paper is completely soaked with paint, which has been absorbed by it.

5- Carefully, since the paper is very delicate at this stage, begin to open the various folds over a table that has been protected with a piece of paper.

6- Let it dry, making sure that it stays completely flat. Once dry, the paper presents diffused colors that create an appealing composition.

chapter

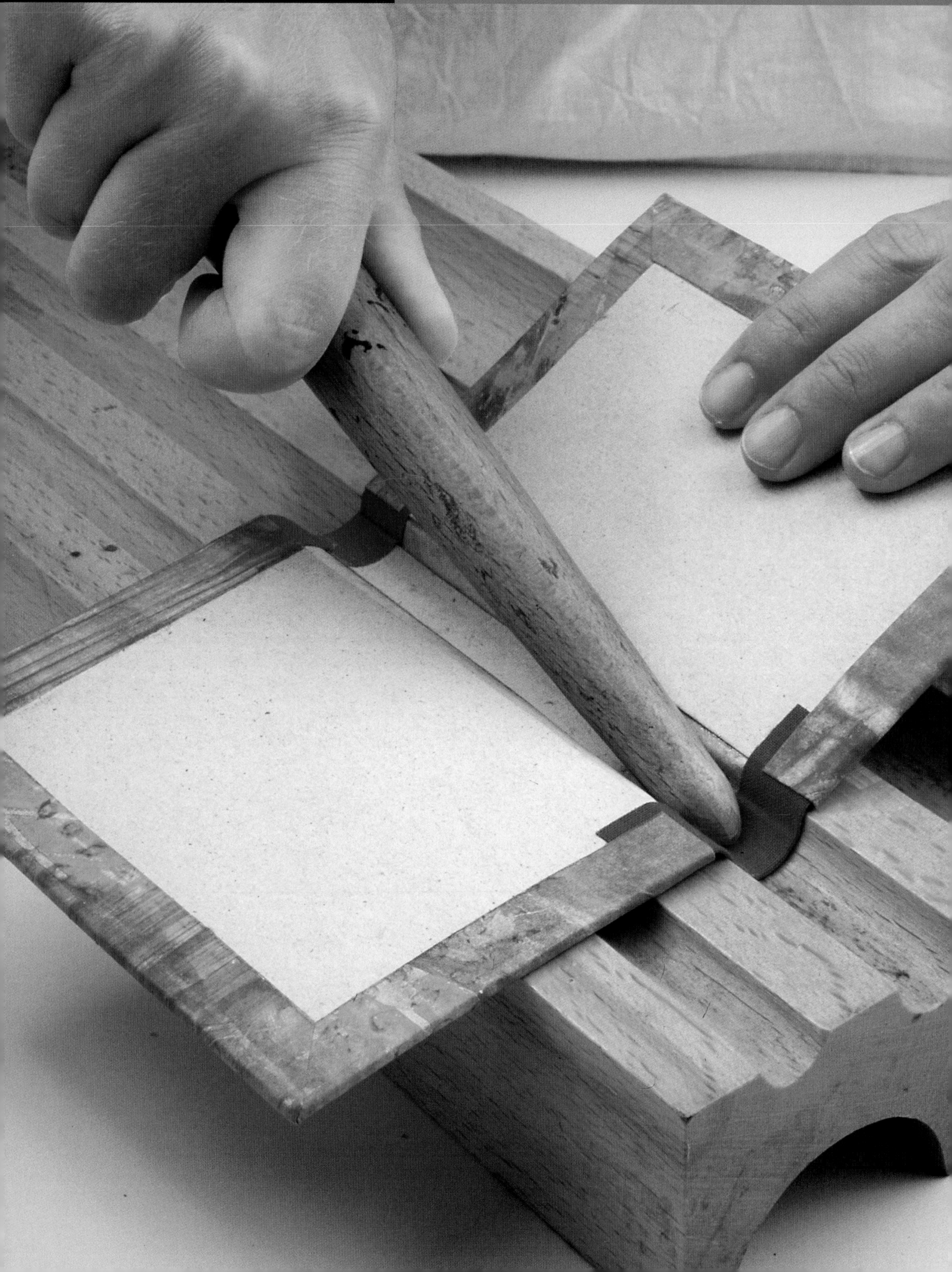

5

Step-by-Step Projects

After going through the history of
bookbinding and explaining the materials,
techniques, and procedures, as well as the different
ways in which paper can be painted, we now tackle a series
of projects that should be executed slowly, step by step, to diffuse
any possible problems.
Some of these projects refer to previous ones because some part is
repeated or begins the same way as one already explained. For this
reason, they are grouped into a compact single block; for example,
booklets whose beginning steps are shared by all of them.
We are certain that the following projects will provide
a good foundation on which to build, allowing you
to create new elements and new forms as needed,
limited only by your imagination.

Portfolio with Flaps

This is a practical device to protect, store, and transport all types of documents. It can be constructed with different materials and may consist of a single piece or several pieces. In this case, the spine and the corners, as well as the interior flaps, are made of black fabric, while the other surfaces are lined with hand-painted paper using the paste technique.

1- Be sure to cut the cardboard a little bit larger than the papers that are to be protected, keeping in mind the interior space needed for the flaps.

2- Glue the fabric, which will be the folder's spine. This should rise ¾ to 1¼ inches (2 to 3 cm) above the surfaces of the board and be ⅝ inch (1.5 cm) longer than them on both sides so that you are able to fold the fabric down.

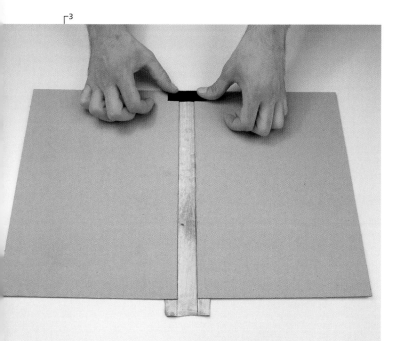

3- This shows how it is folded at the head and tail areas. The central part is covered with glue, so be careful when handling it.

4- Now glue and line the inside of the spine. The fabric must be ¾ inch (2 cm) shorter than the boards and must overlap the side surfaces ⅝ or ¾ inch (1.5 or 2 cm) approximately.

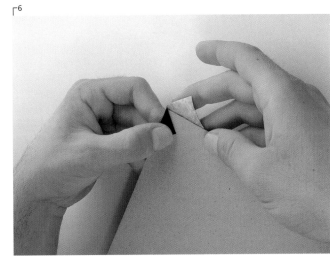

5- The interior fabric is pressed in place with a bone folder or the tip of a finger, trying to avoid any glue blotches or stains.

6- After the two boards are attached at the spine, cut small rectangles out of fabric to make corner protectors, which are glued from outside in.

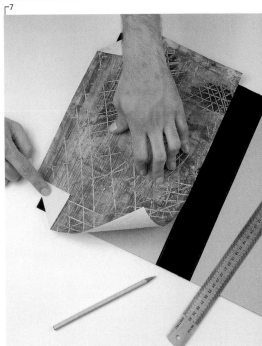

7- To fit in the paper for the panels, distribute it proportionally at the spine and at the borders. First, mark the paper with a pencil, and then measure it, making sure it overhangs ⅝ inch (1.5 cm) on the sides.

8- On the front area, at about ¾ inch (2 cm) from the edge, make a cut to insert the ribbon. If the folder were large, make incisions on the sides as well. To do this you should use a chisel, although a lancet or a craft knife could also work.

9- The ribbon is inserted from the outside with the help of a bone folder (any other thin object could also work). Insert it ⅜ to ¾ inch (1 to 2 cm) and secure it with glue on the inside. You can flatten it with a hammer if it looks too bulgy.

10- Add a pastedown to one of the folder's panels; the other panel will be fitted with a board used to construct the flaps.

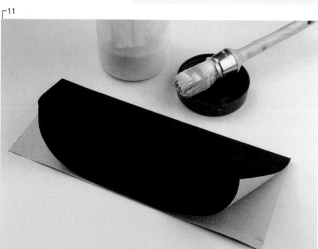

11- A simple way to construct a flap is to use a piece of glued fabric folded over. The double layer of fabric plus the glue form a sufficiently strong body to withstand continuous usage and weight.

12- Cardboard cut to the size of the pastedown, lined with fabric on one side, and three flaps: two for the sides and one for the front. Mark the fabric that goes underneath the board with a pencil and a ruler.

13- Using two sheets of paper as a reference, glue the flap exactly in the area that is marked with the pencil and glue it on the back of the board's pastedown. This way, they will all have the same width.

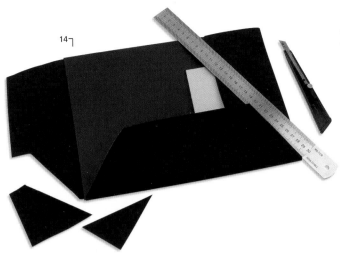

14- When the three flaps have been adhered and the glue is dry, fold them inside the portfolio. Cut them to the desired size and form by placing a board under the flaps and using a ruler and a craft knife.

15- Glue the inside of the board that holds the flaps carefully to avoid staining the fabric, and attach them to the finished portfolio as if it were another pastedown. Once glued, open the flaps and place them under a weight until they are completely dry. This way it will prevent the board from buckling in the future.

16- The finished portfolio holding several papers.

Journal and Case

A journal with a flat spine will be the foundation for a series of projects presented on the following pages. The projects will begin the same way either partially or completely. The case that protects it will also be used repeatedly when we begin making boxes and related objects.

1- Begin with a 27½ × 39½ inch (70 × 100 cm) sheet of good quality paper, and fold and cut in halves until we get a size of approximately 5 × 7 inches (12.5 × 17.5 cm). For this step, use a knife that is not too sharp because we want the edges to be slightly deckled to produce a decorative effect. Take the resulting sheets and, with groups of four sheets, begin to form signatures with a bone folder, making sure they are as evenly folded as possible.

2- Place the signatures between two boards, moving them to the edge of the worktable. Then make four notches with a saw.

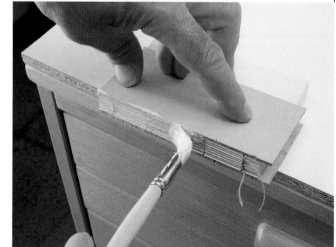

3- Sew the signatures, preferably with an organic twine. Insert the threaded needle through the notches made with the saw, going in and coming out through the next hole, and so on, layering each signature on top of the others (see the section on processes and techniques).

4- Once all the signatures are sewn, place them between two perfectly aligned boards and glue them with a thin layer of thick glue that is spread over the entire spine.

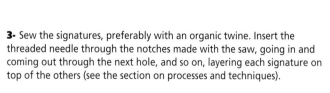

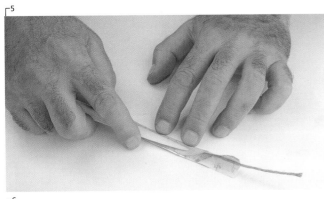

5- Construct the headbands with a piece of color paper, a cord, and the bone folder, as shown in the picture.

6- Glue the headbands on the upper and lower parts of the book and over the spine. Once they are properly secured, shape them with the scissors.

7- Reinforce the spine and the first and last pages by gluing a piece of paper, which will later become the pastedowns. First, attach the paper, which has been previously glued, to the spine, and then attach it carefully to the first and last pages.

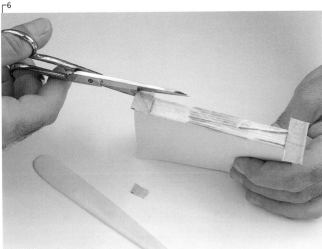

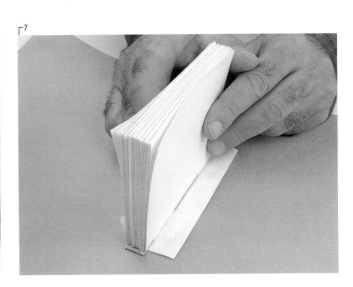

8- Once this is dry, cut out the boards for the covers. These should be ¼ inch (6 mm) longer than the journal and ¾ inch (2 mm) shorter than its width. The spine should be as long as the covers and as wide as the thickness of the journal plus two boards (the thickness of the journal should be measured from the side, not from the spine, which will be somewhat larger as a result of the sewing).

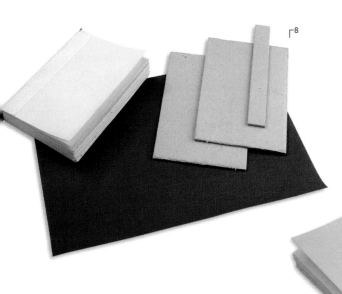

9- Glue the fabric, which should be ⅝ inches (1.5 cm) larger than the boards for the covers. Place them over ³⁄₁₆ inch (9 mm) away from the spine; using a piece of construction paper of these dimensions will make the work easier. Once the boards are in place, cut out the tips and fold the edges.

10- Center the journal on the cover, paying attention to the head, tail, and front, and glue the pastedown with liquid glue. Adjust the covers to make sure that they are even with each other. Then, glue the other pastedown the same way. The spine will be left unglued to give the book more flexibility when opening.

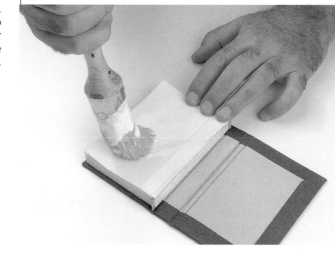

11- Immediately after that, place the book in the press between wood boards, making sure the spine is left exposed. Once the journal is properly centered, apply pressure. A few seconds later, remove it to check if it is completely glued, and then place it under a weight for a few hours.

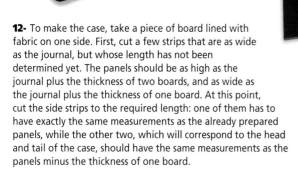

12- To make the case, take a piece of board lined with fabric on one side. First, cut a few strips that are as wide as the journal, but whose length has not been determined yet. The panels should be as high as the journal plus the thickness of two boards, and as wide as the journal plus the thickness of one board. At this point, cut the side strips to the required length: one of them has to have exactly the same measurements as the already prepared panels, while the other two, which will correspond to the head and tail of the case, should have the same measurements as the panels minus the thickness of one board.

13- Insert a ribbon through the surface of the board, from inside out, with the help of a craft knife. Glue is applied to the end that is left outside. Begin to construct the case with thick glue, first the sides, over the base, and then the second panel, which will cover the case.

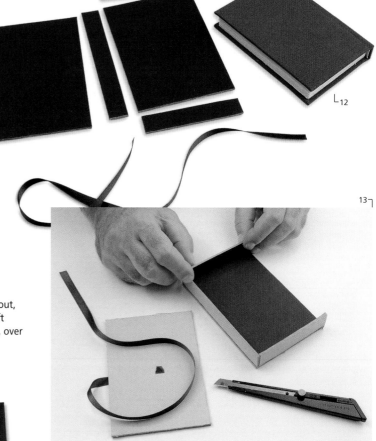

14- Once the case has been put together, cut the fabric that will line it. Fold ⅝ inch (1.5 cm) inward at the mouth of the case; on the sides, try to pull the fabric just about half the width of the journal to avoid overlapping, which could cause unnecessary bulging. In addition to the panels, cut the sides. The fabric for the top and the bottom should come ⅝ inch (1.5 cm) inside the opening and fold slightly over the back; the piece of fabric for the back must measure exactly the height of the case.

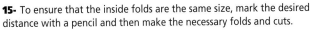

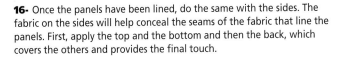

15- To ensure that the inside folds are the same size, mark the desired distance with a pencil and then make the necessary folds and cuts.

16- Once the panels have been lined, do the same with the sides. The fabric on the sides will help conceal the seams of the fabric that line the panels. First, apply the top and the bottom and then the back, which covers the others and provides the final touch.

17- View of the finished journal and case.

Travel Journal

This is a classic journal in Europe and in America. It has been manufactured in small shops for two hundred years and later sold in stationary and specialty stores. It is basically a travel journal with room for many things. The elastic band is an important feature to close it and to secure its contents, and the small pocket in the front can be useful for holding cards and small objects.

1- Use sheets of previously sewn paper, lightweight boards, black paper, and imitation leather or a non-porous material that can withstand heavy use.

2- Cut out a couple of pastedowns, preferably black and glue them up to the edge of the spine with a thin layer of glue ¾ inch (2 cm) wide.

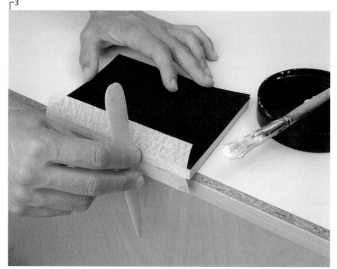

3- Once you are sure that all the pages of the journal are perfectly aligned at the spine and at the top and bottom parts, apply a thin layer of glue over the signatures. It should have thick consistency and be thoroughly spread. Place a small piece of percale on the spine, leaving between ⅝ and ¾ inches (1.5 and 2 cm) of material unglued.

4- When dry, cut all three sides with the guillotine. Round off the front corners with a small cut and even them out with sandpaper. Obviously, there are machines that can do these tasks, but because of their size and cost, it is unrealistic to have one at home.

5- Cut two thin boards exactly the same size as the journal. Do this with a craft knife and round off the corners with scissors.

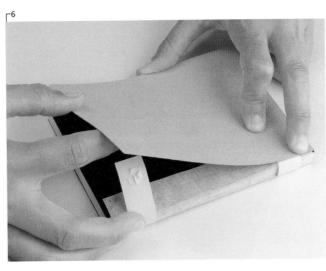

6- Attach the board pieces to the journal. Glue a strip of paper, as shown in the picture, to know exactly the distance that should be left between the boards for the spine to fit.

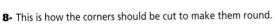

7- Glue the two covers on the material (imitation leather in this case), leaving ⅝ inch (1.5 cm) extra on all sides. Notice how the pieces of paper placed before prevent any measurement errors.

8- This is how the corners should be cut to make them round.

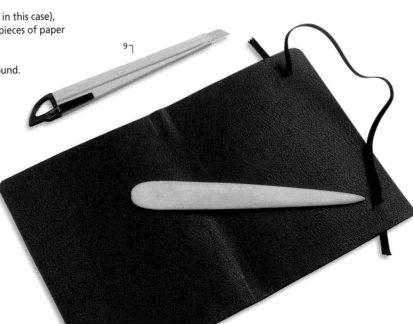

9- Once the materials have been folded over the cover, remove the paper that held the two boards together and make a cut with the craft knife at ⅝ inch (1.5 cm) from the outside corners of one of the covers. Insert an elastic band, which was prepared beforehand, through the cut and glue it inside. This elastic should be loose because it will have to go around the journal and close it tightly.

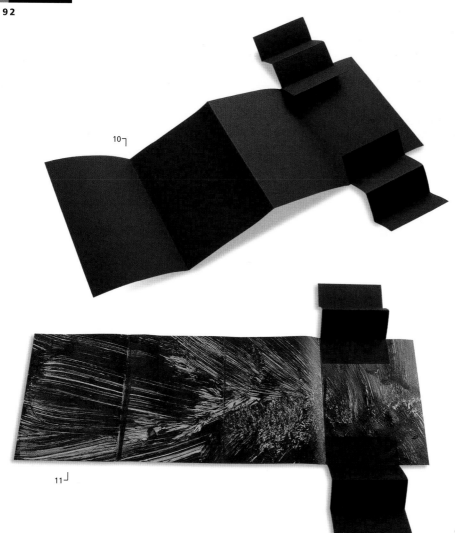

10-

10- Take a piece of black paper, which after being folded four times will be the size of the journal. You will use it to make a small pocket at the back of the journal. Now put two small pieces of paper together and make four folds with them as shown in the illustration; these will be the springs for the pocket.

11-

11- After applying glue all over the large paper, adhere the small pieces on the first quarter.

12-

⌐13

12- This is how the paper is folded on itself. The sides and the last of the four folds are not adhered yet.

13- Glue the last of the sides and the last fold of the large paper over it. This way you will construct a pocket with a spring, which you will put aside to dry and save for later use.

14- Glue the pastedowns as usual, centering them over the covers. When pressed, the elastic band should be moved away from the cover and a piece of medium weight board should be placed between them to make sure that the elastic does not leave an imprint on the panels.

15- Now you only have to glue the small pockets over the pastedown that conceals the elastic band. The pocket should open in the direction of the book's spine; otherwise, the objects inside of it could fall out.

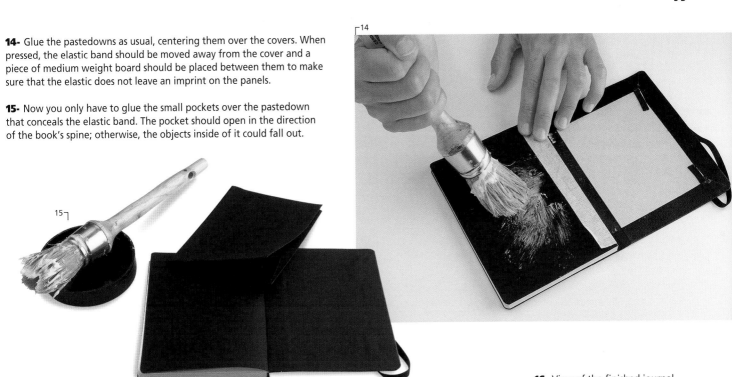

16- View of the finished journal.

Bradel-Binding Booklet

This type of binding dates back to the eighteenth century. It consists of three pieces (the spine and the two panels), and its large hollow allows the book to open wide. Due to its durability, it was used for many years to store heavily used documents. Nowadays, many photo albums and certain books of special characteristics are made this way. Its shape allows the use of a variety of materials. In this specific case, we will use fabric and paper, which has been painted beforehand with the paste method.

1- Sewn booklet (same as the one in pages 86 to 89), painted paper, fabric, and light and medium weight boards.

2- Glue the pastedowns to the booklet, which is already sewn and glued at the spine, being careful not to stain the first and last pages.

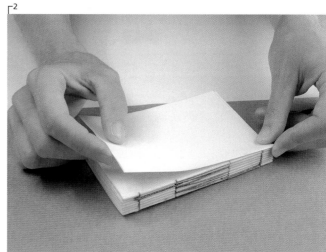

3- Then, placing the book at the guillotine, trim off the front part.

4- Hammer the spine to make it round, holding the front part with one hand.

5- Apply glue with a brush to the headbands and to the lining paper for the spine. This would have been glued separately, and should be adhered to the spine and over the top and bottom pastedowns.

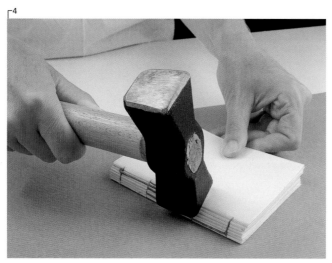

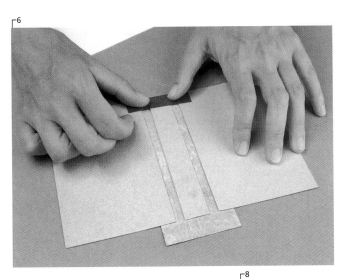

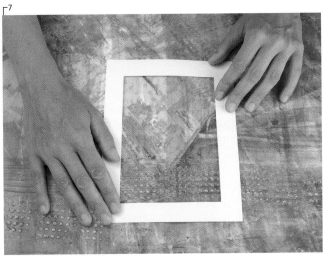

6- To make the covers, cut two boards of each weight, exactly the same size: ¼ inch (6 mm) longer than the book and ⅜ to ¾ inches (1 to 2 cm) shorter than its width. The height of the spine should be the same as the covers and its width with the rounded width of the spine plus the thickness of the other four boards. Attach the spine and the two thin boards with the fabric, leaving a ¼ to ⁵⁄₁₆ inch (6 to 8 mm) channel.

7- With the help of a window made out of cardboard, select the area of the paper that you like the most to make the panels.

8- Once the panels have been cut out, glue them, using a paper that has been placed there to protect the surface of the table.

9- Place the board over the glued part and fold the paper over, only on the side that will be the spine.

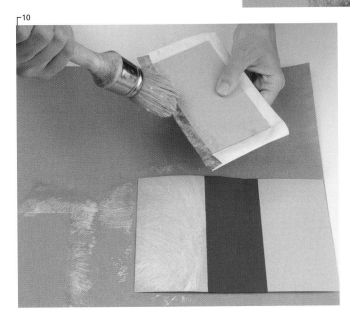

10- The three pieces that form the binding are ready now. To bind them together, glue the surfaces of the thick board but avoid staining the fabric. Proceed the same way with the edge of the cover already lined.

11- This is how the two planes are attached. After keeping the book under weight, glue the edges and fold them over.

12- Shape the spine with a spine rounding form.

13- After mounting the pages inside the covers, attach the pastedowns carefully so that the book can open wide.

14- The finished book.

Photo Album

This photo album is a unique piece that is easy to make. Before preparing the materials, it is important to decide how many photos it will hold. The size must also be decided so the paper can be cut to the required dimensions. You can customize this piece completely according to your needs: it can be for a certain trip, a specific vacation period, or a celebration.

1- Cardboard pieces measuring approximately 10 × 13¾ inches (25 × 35 cm), fabric, paper, and cardboard risers ½ to ⅝ inch (12 to 15 mm) wide and ⅝ to ¾ inch (1.5 to 2 cm) less in length than the cardboard sheets.

2- Make a mark with the bone folder at ⅛ inch (3 mm) from the edges of the papers. The thickness of the ruler can be used as the measurement, and a piece of soft cardboard placed under the paper will make things easier.

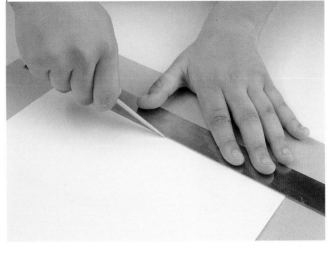

3- Place the papers between two boards, line them up on the side of the markings, and place them under a weight. You will have previously decided on the number of risers needed, depending on how thick the photographs are. Begin to insert them from the spine one by one and attach to the edge of the sheets. Then, they will be attached with thick glue.

4- Cut two strips of fabric somewhat shorter than the sheets and 2 to 2⅜ inches (5 to 6 cm) wide. You will need the two risers that have been put aside, and a box of nails no longer than the thickness of the spine.

5- Place the reverse side of the fabric over the album and place the riser, adhered with a couple dots of glue, over the fabric. Insert five nails on each side, making sure that they are straight and that they do not stick out.

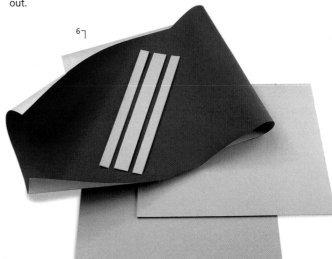

6- The boards for the covers should be the same height as the album plus ⅜ inch (1 cm); its width should be the same as that of the cover minus ³⁄₁₆ inch (0.5 cm). Once prepared to size, cut ⅝ inches (1.5 cm) from the side that touches the spine and save the four strips. Cut the fabric with a ¾ inch (2 cm) overhang on each side. The spine should have the height of the panels and the width of the spine plus two boards.

7- This is how the upper and lower finishes are constructed with a board and fabric. This finish will conceal the risers that are visible through the sheets.

8- After gluing the fabric, attach the board that corresponds to the album's surface. Place the reserved strip at ⅜ inch (1 cm) from this followed by the spine, at a distance that includes the thickness of one and a half boards. Then, at the same distance and after the spine, attach the second strip and the second panel. After gluing the spine and the two sides, mount the cover.

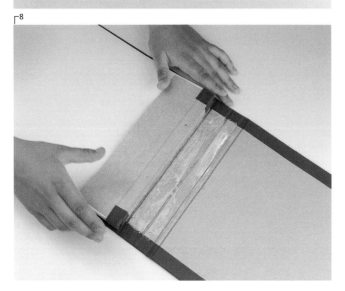

9- Keep some extra paper between the fabric and the first page, then glue and adhere the fabric to the inside of the cover.

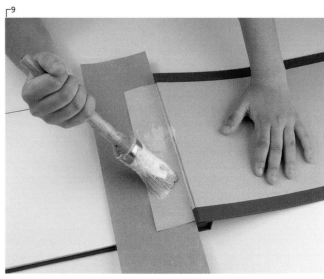

10- Line the panels with a piece of patterned paper cut to size, and fold the edges over.

11- The pastedowns can be cut from the same paper as the pages, somewhat smaller than the latter to prevent them from sticking out the sides.

12- View of the finished album.

Book with Ribbons and Exposed Sewing

This is an interesting book in which the ribbons serve as the binding and decoration at the same time. The thread used for sewing and the pastedowns are also ornamental elements in which color plays a very important role, since different materials are combined to form a single piece. This book is constructed without any glue on the spine, which is why it can be opened wide.

1- Ribbon, embroidery floss, good quality hand-made paper of considerable weight, plus thin paper for the pastedowns are all the basic materials needed to make this book.

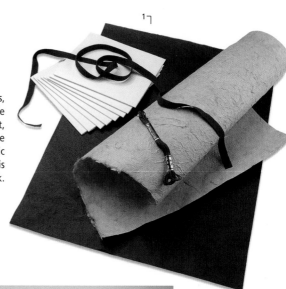

2- After notching the spine as needed, sew the book with the ribbons and the same color thread.

3- Place the pastedowns on the upper and lower parts of the book, using the thin paper.

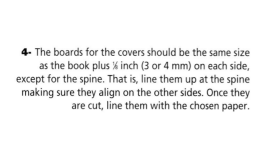

4- The boards for the covers should be the same size as the book plus ⅛ inch (3 or 4 mm) on each side, except for the spine. That is, line them up at the spine making sure they align on the other sides. Once they are cut, line them with the chosen paper.

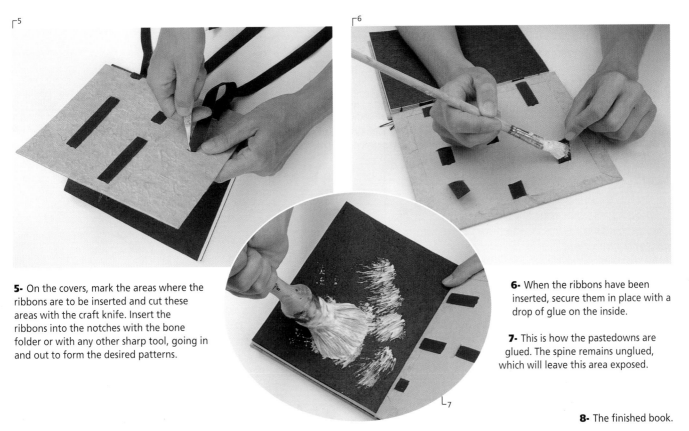

5- On the covers, mark the areas where the ribbons are to be inserted and cut these areas with the craft knife. Insert the ribbons into the notches with the bone folder or with any other sharp tool, going in and out to form the desired patterns.

6- When the ribbons have been inserted, secure them in place with a drop of glue on the inside.

7- This is how the pastedowns are glued. The spine remains unglued, which will leave this area exposed.

8- The finished book.

Book with Flap and Closure

For this project, a medieval book with simple materials will be made. Most of the materials used to be made of leather or parchment paper, but in this case we are going to use a simple cloth prepared for binding.

You will begin with one signature or sheet, although the same procedure would be applicable for any book, booklet, or magazine.

This same booklet with interior flaps could be used for storing a letter, a drawing, or a document, giving it a distinguished look.

2- Make three holes with an awl in the center of the sheet of paper, one in the middle and two on each side.

3- Insert a threaded needle from the outside starting at the center and then pull it through the upper hole. Finally, insert the needle in the bottom hole and pull it around through the center hole, which is the starting point. With the twine pulled taut make a knot with the two ends.

4- Place the covers at the beginning and at the end of the booklet.

1- Sheets of paper to make the signature, lightweight board, fabric, a strip of chamois, and a piece of parchment paper are the materials needed to begin.

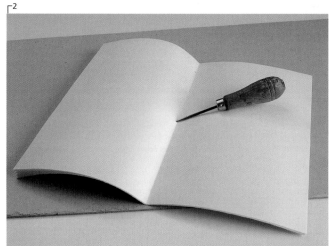

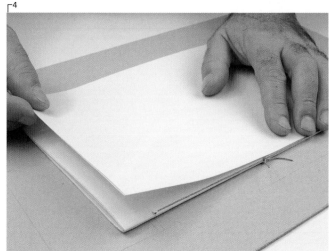

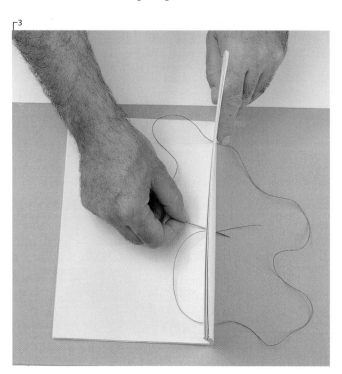

5- A 1½ inches-wide (4 cm) piece of paper or fabric cut on the bias reinforces the spine.

6- Cut the board for the covers ⅜ inch (8 mm) higher than the booklet and about ⅜ inch (8 mm) less in width. The flap is cut as shown in the picture, without going over one third of the book's width.

7- This is an important part of the binding process, which will determine its success. Center both panels over the booklet, with one on top and one on the bottom, leaving a wider margin in the front.
Hold it in place and glue two strips of paper on the back of the board: one on top and one on the bottom.

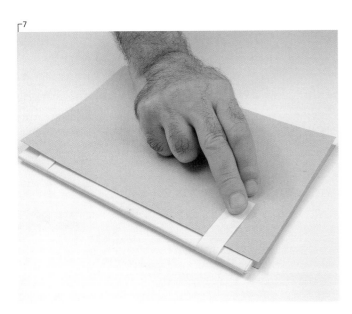

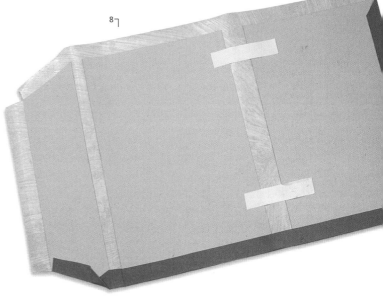

8- View of the cover half way through. The distance from the spine is given; however, it is a good idea that the one that goes from the flap to the board be somewhat larger than the thickness of the book (between ¼ and ⅜ inches) (0.5 and 1 cm).

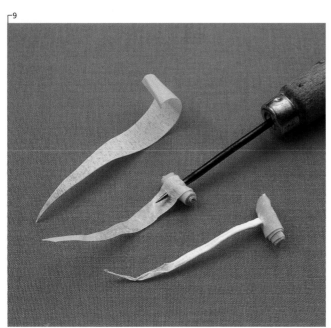

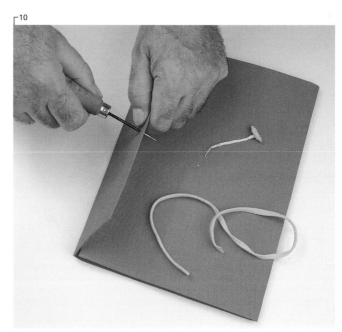

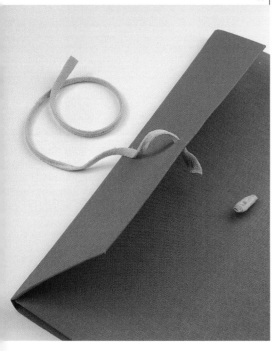

9- This is how to make a button out of parchment paper. Cut a cone out of parchment paper and begin folding it over, starting at the wide part and working toward the narrow part. Make a hole with an awl and insert the narrow end through it. Simply tug on the end that sticks out and it is finished.

10- Make a hole in the center of the flap with an awl at ⅝ inches (1.5 cm) from the edge and another one approximately in the center of the cover's board.

11- Insert the thin strip of chamois through the hole on the flap, and the parchment button through the other one.

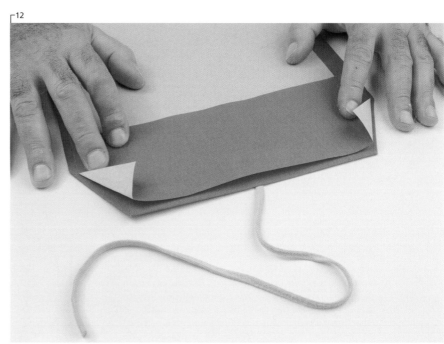

12- Cut a pattern out of fabric to cover the inside of the flap, letting it extend ⅝ inches (1.5 cm) over the panel.

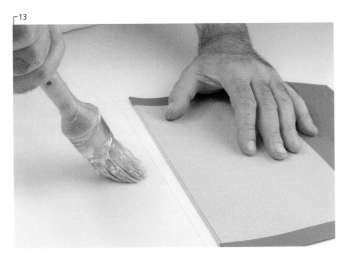

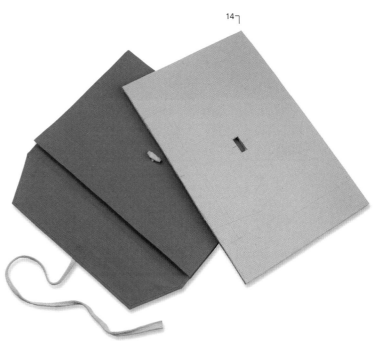

13- Glue the part of the fabric that connects both panels and insert the booklet, completely centered. When it dries, glue the pastedowns.

14- To place the book in the press without damaging the parchment button, take a larger piece of cardboard and make a hole in the center, which will line up with the button.
Place it in the press like this, between two wood boards, for a few seconds and then place a weight over it until it dries.

15- A perfectly finished binding.

Japanese-Style Book

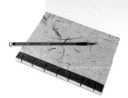

This is one of the many sewing techniques used for books. This type of sewing in particular can be used for catalogs, magazines, and booklets in general, since it is very practical and elegant due to its simplicity and strong finish.

We should mention that each page is doubled because this book was originally made out of rice paper, which absorbs ink easily. This way, people could write or draw with ink and a reed pen without fear of smearing the previous page.

1- Several sheets of paper to make the book, handmade Japanese paper, somewhat heavier paper to give it body, and twine for sewing, in this case embroidery floss that matches the colors of the paper are needed.

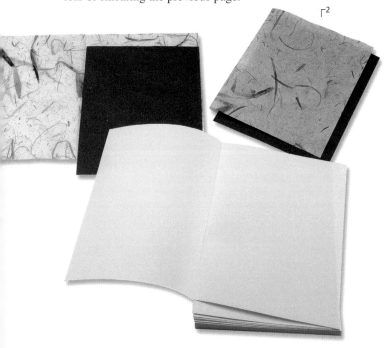

2- Cut out the paper to the desired size, since it cannot be cut at the guillotine later. Also, cut the paper that goes inside the covers to the same size. Finally, the outside paper will be doubled and will adorn the cover on both sides by forming a sheet that will envelope the paper previously cut.

3- Glue a piece of paper next to the spine. This is done on both sides to reinforce the first pages from the sewing.

4- Mark the location of the holes for the sewing with a divider. Keep in mind that the side that is cut corresponds to the spine, while the folded side should be the front.

5- Traditionally, the holes were made with an awl, but nowadays there is a machine fitted with a thin drill bit that makes this operation easier and more exact.

6- Beginning at the center (see the section on processes and techniques), sew the book with the embroidery floss.

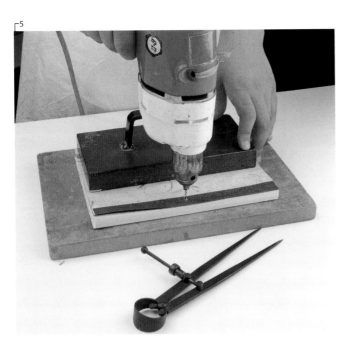

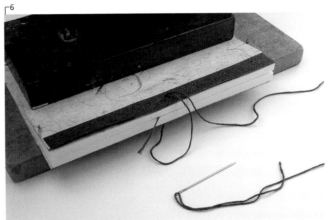

7- View of the finished book.

Box with a Detached Lid

This project begins a section that deals with boxes. Independent of the protection that documents and prints deserve, a great variety of objects like card holders, pencil holders, trays for paper clips and erasers, and more can also benefit from this process. A box is a very practical object but it can be decorative by itself.

1- Heavy cardboard and papers with different characteristics are the basis needed to build this box.

2 and 3- When the paper is very thin or very porous, as is the case of Japanese paper, you will need to apply another sheet of paper to add consistency. The procedure involves applying glue carefully to a sheet of paper that is similar in size to the one made by hand, making sure that no bubbles are formed while the glue is being applied. Then, the patterned paper is placed over the heavier sheet of paper, extending it completely. To prevent the paper from buckling while applying the glue, hold it in place with several pins on the corners.

4- The first step in making the box is to cut a base and four sides. The sides should be as wide as the box is high, as for the length, two sides should be as long as the base. The other two should be the width of the base minus the thickness of two boards. Once they are cut, place them over a paper in the configuration of the interior of the box.

5- When the paper is a little bit dry, cut it to the size of the boards using a craft knife.

6- Apply thick glue to the sides of the boards and begin to assemble it. For this step, it is preferable for the boards and the paper not to be completely dry otherwise they would buckle, which would make the assembly more difficult.

7- First, line the two longest sides with paper. The paper for this procedure is 1¼ inch (3 cm) longer and wider than the sides themselves, so the paper, when applied, will exceed ⅝ inch (1.5 cm) on all sides. A vertical slit at the corner will allow the paper to be folded inside the box.

8- At the base, the cut is bigger so the amount of paper to be folded over is as small as possible.

9- The two remaining sides should be as high as the box plus 1¼ inch (3 cm), and as wide as the box minus the thickness of two boards, to make mounting them easier.

10- Obviously, the base should be a bit smaller than the box to avoid excess paper on the sides. This concludes the first part of the exercise.

11- Begin with cutting and assembling the lid. It should be a little bit larger than the box, because the box must fit inside the lid. First, measure the lid and add the thickness of one board to it on all sides, plus a bit more for the thickness of the paper. Assemble the boards without the lining inside. With a piece of paper measure the height of the side plus approximately ⅜ inch (1 cm) that will be folded over.

12- The resulting dimension is the paper that should overhang on all sides of the lid, when it is cut to size.

13- Once the glue has been applied to the paper, center the lid on it and cut it as shown in the picture.

14- This is how we proceed with the folds and cuts. First, fold the long sides, leaving the short sides, which can be folded without cutting.

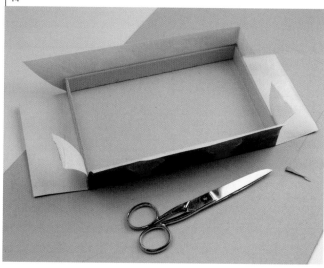

15- Cut the lining paper to size for the interior of the box and glue it, making sure it adheres completely.

16- The finished box. In addition to being a practical container, the box and the lid can be used separately as desk accessories.

Continuous Protective Case

People always have pictures, magazines, and documents that need to be kept together on a shelf or protected in a drawer. This box, assembled in a way that the body and the lid form a single piece, can be very practical for this purpose. Because of its format, it can be stored vertically on a bookshelf or flat in a drawer. A label with its contents can be added to the book's spine or to its front panel.

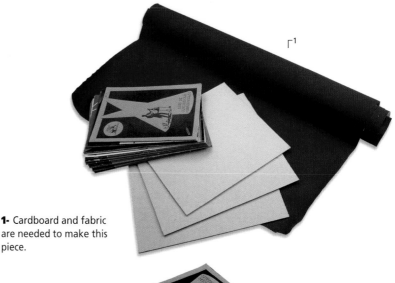

1- Cardboard and fabric are needed to make this piece.

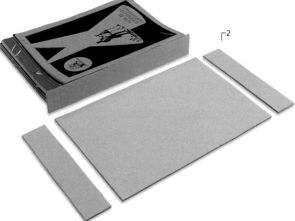

2- First, cut three sides, taking into account the thickness of the magazines that will be stored in it, and a length that it is still undetermined. The cardboard for the base has to be as long as the longest magazine, plus the thickness of two boards (the side ones that we have cut are a reference to take the measurements). To define the width, take the widest magazine as a reference and add to this the thickness of one board. After cutting the base, add the sides to it. The long one should be exactly the size of the base, while the two small ones, the width of the base minus the thickness of one board.

3- Once all the boards are prepared, glue them, making sure that the long side overlaps the first one and that the two small ones are fitted accordingly.

4- To make the second box, proceed in the same way we did when we made the first box with respect to the magazines that were to be stored in it. Because the second box is made just like the first one, you must first cut the sides, and then the base, which must have the same height as the first box plus the thickness of two boards and the width of the first one plus the thickness of one board. The side pieces are sized to the base and then attached to it.

5- When the two boxes have been assembled, cut the spine. It must be as wide as the large box and the same length.

6- Use a paper to measure the large box. Get the width of the inner and outer side pieces plus ⅜ inch (1 cm) that will be folded over inside the box.

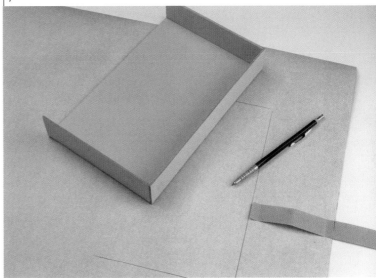

7- To cut the fabric that will line the case, proceed as follows: place the two boxes with the spine between them as if you were going to assemble them. Then, allow for the measurements that you took before on all four sides.

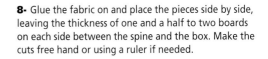

8- Glue the fabric on and place the pieces side by side, leaving the thickness of one and a half to two boards on each side between the spine and the box. Make the cuts free hand or using a ruler if needed.

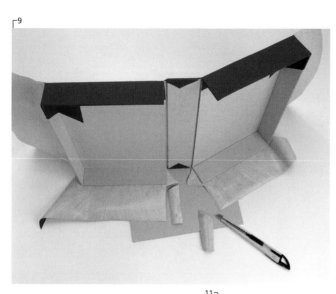

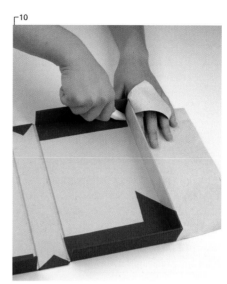

9- This is how the sides should be cut to fold them over inside the box.

10- After cutting the edges, begin folding over the sides. Adjust the corners with the bone folder trying to conceal the board with the fabric.

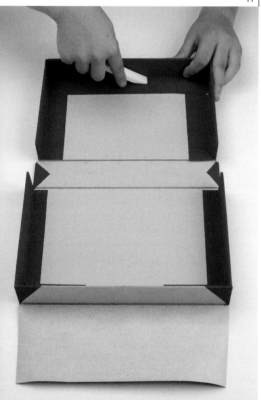

11- Finally, fold the side pieces that have not been cut. If they are dry because too much time has elapsed, apply another layer of glue. This prevents you from rushing the work.

12- It is a good idea to include a cardboard reinforcement on each panel. In addition to enhancing the shape of the case, they provide an even surface for the interior lining.

13- The inside lining is cut in a single piece. Initially, take the largest part as a reference. Once a perfect rectangle has been cut out, add to it a small ledge on the side of the smaller box, so it can fit inside without a problem.

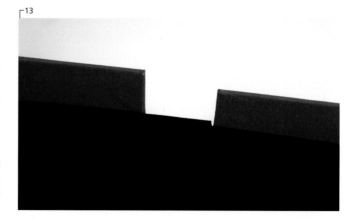

14- After applying glue to the backside of the paper or fabric that lines the interior, adhere it, beginning with the small part first and continue pressing, making sure no bubbles are formed. To adjust the edges use a bone folder.

15- Once dry, you can pack the objects you wanted to protect and close the case. It is ready for storage.

Case in Book Format with Flat Spine

This project is a response to our need to individualize a book, whether it is new or old. It can also be a solution to provide protection, to make something unique, to give as a present, or to provide personal enjoyment. Using this technique, you can keep the original edition without the need for a new binding. As with a previous project, you can add the title of the book to the spine or to the front panel with a label, playing with the decorative elements so that it can be incorporated as a part of the design.

1- The book that needs protecting and the basic material needed for it: boards, fabric, and papers.

2- Mark the thickness of the book on a board, allowing for extra space; ⅝ to ¾ inch (1.5 to 2 cm) are enough, keeping this in mind when you are ready to line it later with fabric or paper.

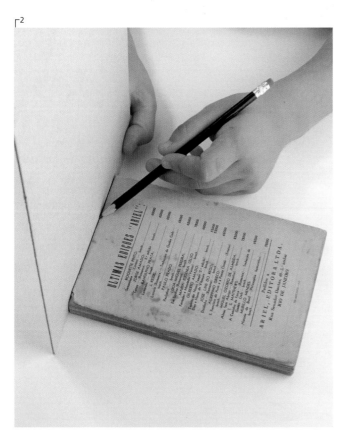

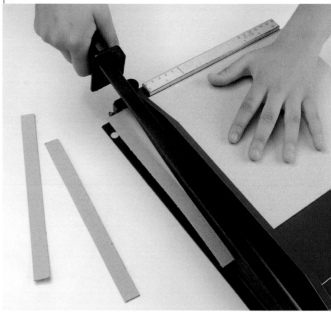

3- With a sheer, cut the three cardboard strips with the previously established dimensions. Also cut the base of the box, which should be as long as the book plus the thickness of a board. Once the base is cut adjust the side pieces. The long side should be as long as the base, while the two short ones have to be as wide as the base minus the thickness of one board.

4- Apply a little bit of glue and begin assembling. Glue the small sides over the base, which in turn will be glued to the long side piece.

5- With a strip of paper, measure the inner and outer part of one of the sides, allowing extra ⅜ inch (1 cm) approximately on each side.

6- The measurement taken before will be used now to cut three pieces of fabric of that width, the height being that of the box.

7- First, line the short sides. To do this, glue one of the pieces leaving ⅜ inch (1 cm) under the base and the rest above.

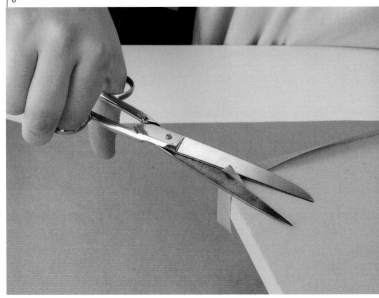

8- When the fabric is folded over the longest side, make the first cut on the under side of the base. This should almost be flat so the fabric will not overlap too much.

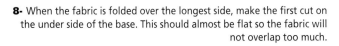

9- The cut on the upper side has to be vertical, thus cutting the smallest amount of fabric possible, so when the sides are folded inwards they do not leave any part of the board visible.

10- This is how the part of the case that does not have the long side should be cut, to ensure that the fabric presents a perfect finish.

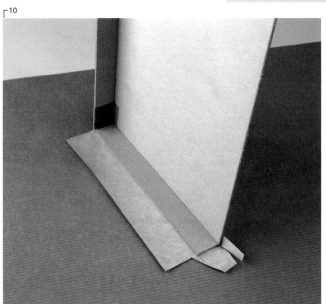

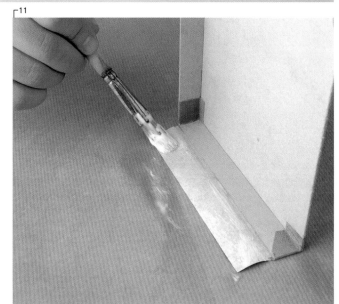

11- Once the two small flaps are folded over, fold the large one. Press it tight against the board to prevent bubbles from forming on the folds. If the glue has dried out, you can apply a second layer.

12- Line the interior of the box with a fabric cut exactly to size, except for the part that will fold inward about ⅝ inch (1.5 cm).

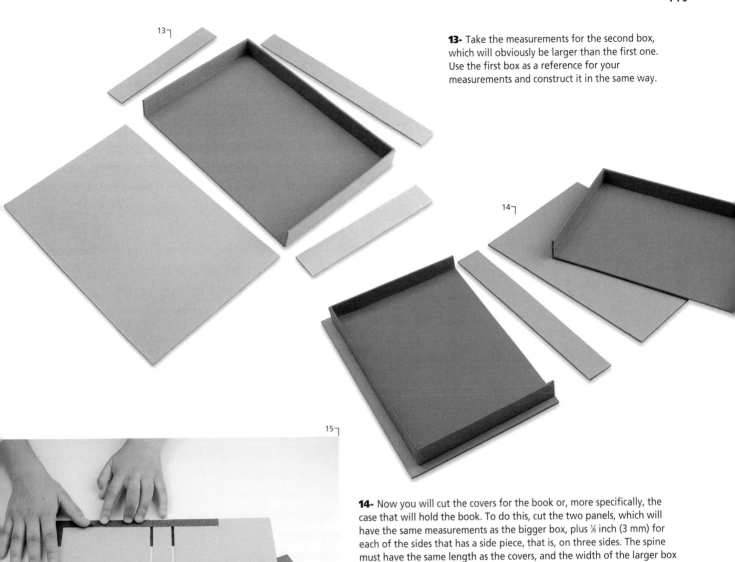

13- Take the measurements for the second box, which will obviously be larger than the first one. Use the first box as a reference for your measurements and construct it in the same way.

14- Now you will cut the covers for the book or, more specifically, the case that will hold the book. To do this, cut the two panels, which will have the same measurements as the bigger box, plus ⅛ inch (3 mm) for each of the sides that has a side piece, that is, on three sides. The spine must have the same length as the covers, and the width of the larger box plus the thickness of the two panels of the box.

15- Arrange the pieces according to the measurements and begin assembling the lid, leaving a space equal to the thickness of one and a half to two boards between each panel and spine.

16- Continue assembling the lid with the colors and textures previously chosen, matching them with the colors of the book that you want to protect.

17- When the exterior is finished, attach a piece of fabric on the inside of the spine. This will be visible; therefore, you should make sure that its color goes well with the colors of the boxes.

18- To conceal the folded pieces of the cover, add a pastedown on the inside of it. If this is not enough, adhere a second one on top when the first one is dry.

19- The spine is set at a 90-degree angle to the panel of the lid and mounted on the small box. While you set it against the spine, adjust it to make sure that the three flaps fit within the panel. Use thick glue to adhere it.

20- Place it under a weight for drying.

21- Now, glue the second box the same way you did the first one. Put it inside the latter and let the lid's panel fall inside of it. A few minutes later, open it carefully and place it under a weight until it is completely dry.

22- The book placed inside the case. Notice how the colors of the book complement the colors of the case perfectly.

22⌐

23⌐

23- View of the exterior of the case. The title can be printed or written in calligraphy on the panel or the spine.

Case in Book Format with Round Spine

This is a variation of the previous project. A round spine provides a different finish as well as a series of possibilities to create other objects like boxes, folders, or covers. Besides holding the book, as in the previous exercise, it can be used for postcards, newspaper clippings, magazines, and so on. Its format makes it blend perfectly when placed on the shelf with books.

1- Painted paper, fabric, board pieces, and a rounded wood spine that can vary depending on the thickness.

2- As in the previous project, assemble two boxes with fabric, which will become the inside of this "book case." Two thick boards will become the lids.

3- To cut the lids make sure that the boards are ⅛ inch (3 mm) longer than the larger box on every side. That is, three sides on the upper part, three sides on the lower part, and three on the front. The spine will be flush with the box. Once the lids are cut to size, proceed to cut a piece of cardboard that will become the reinforcement for the spine. This should be as long as the larger box, and as wide as the width of the large box plus the thickness of the boards for the lids.

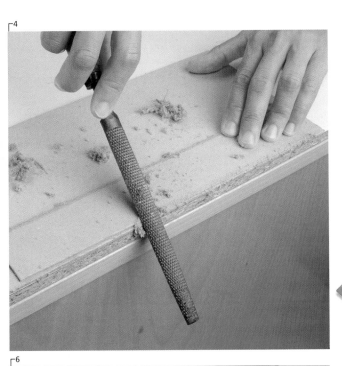

4- Place this piece on a board against the edge of a table. Shape it with a rasp to a 45-degree angle and then file it with sandpaper.

5- Cut the strip of wood the same length as the board trimmed on the sides.

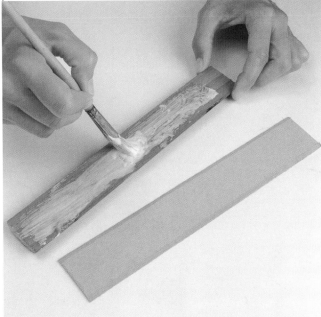

6- The wood should never be wider than the board, but it can be quite a bit narrower. Apply glue to the wood with a brush, making sure it is perfectly distributed, and adhere it to the board. Leave it to dry under a weight.

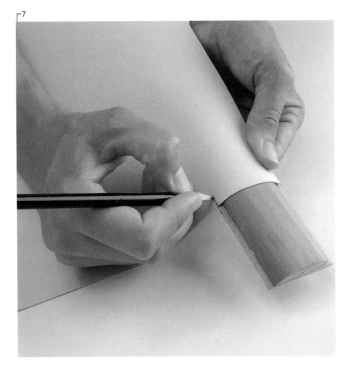

7- With a piece of lightweight cardboard measure the distance from one edge of the board to the other, going over the piece of wood. Cut it and adjust it to the same height.

8- File the edges of the board with sandpaper, and then shape it with a spine rounding form.

9- Apply thick glue to it and place it over the wood. If the wood is small with respect to the board, there would be pockets of air on the sides, and you may have to glue another piece of cardboard over the first one to give it more consistency.

10- This is how the constructed piece is lined with fabric. The long sides are folded over without touching each other; however, the upper and lower parts are left flush without folding.

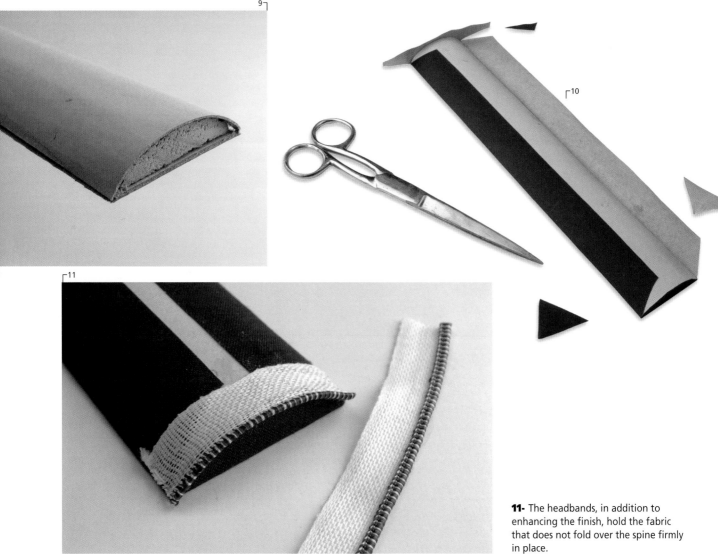

11- The headbands, in addition to enhancing the finish, hold the fabric that does not fold over the spine firmly in place.

12- Putting aside the piece that will become the inside of the spine, continue constructing the covers, which have already been cut. Make a 45-degree angle cut on the upper and lower parts of the spine.

13- Now the spine must be cut. To do this, take a cardboard of the same length as the covers and of the width of the piece that will form the inside of the rounded area. Once cut, sand the covers and the spine with a rasp and finish them off with sandpaper. Sand the covers on the three sides that are not the spine, and the spine only on its edges, leaving the upper and lower parts intact.

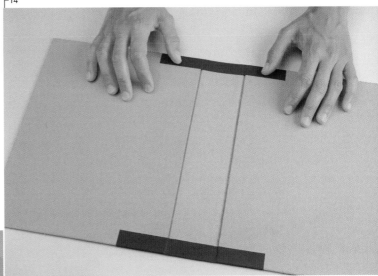

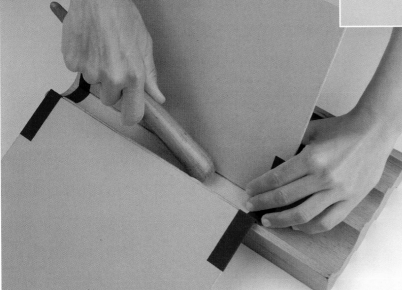

14- Mount the fabric that will hold the three pieces together. Glue it on the flat pieces one third of its width, leaving a 1/16 to 1/8 inch (2 to 3 mm) space between the spine and the cardboard for the cover.

15- Round off the spine with the rounding form to fit inside the piece that you had put aside.

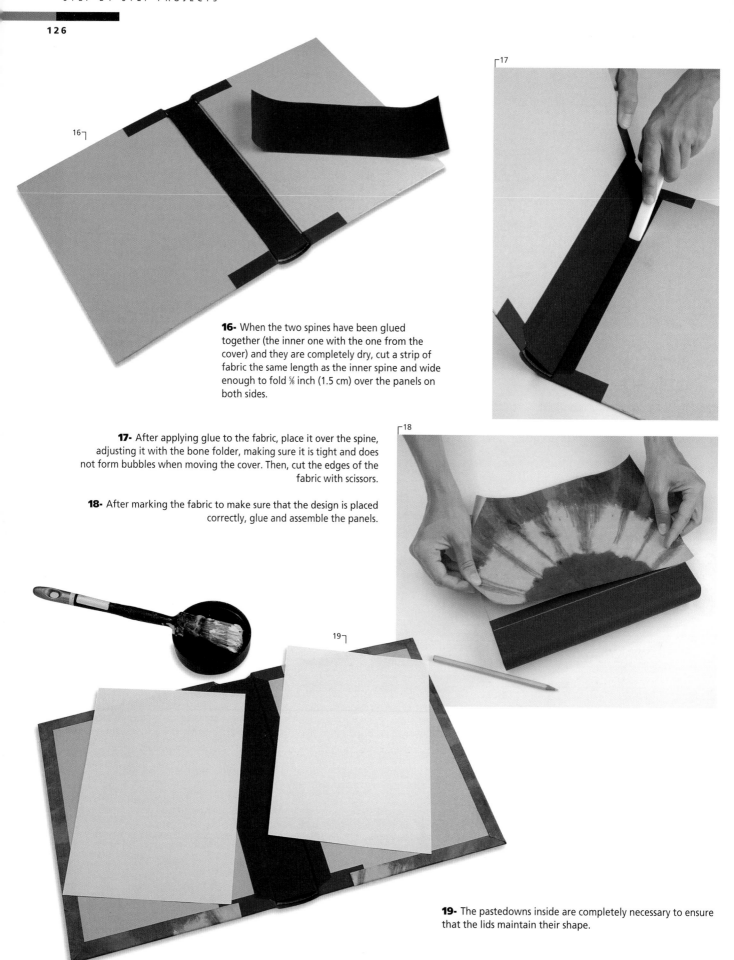

16- When the two spines have been glued together (the inner one with the one from the cover) and they are completely dry, cut a strip of fabric the same length as the inner spine and wide enough to fold ⅝ inch (1.5 cm) over the panels on both sides.

17- After applying glue to the fabric, place it over the spine, adjusting it with the bone folder, making sure it is tight and does not form bubbles when moving the cover. Then, cut the edges of the fabric with scissors.

18- After marking the fabric to make sure that the design is placed correctly, glue and assemble the panels.

19- The pastedowns inside are completely necessary to ensure that the lids maintain their shape.

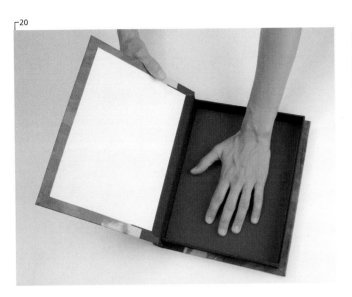

20- Apply glue to the small box aligning it with the spine and allowing the same overhang on all three sides. Put a weight over it and let it dry.

21- Place the large box over the small one, apply glue, and after adjusting the cover on its surface, let it dry.

22- View of the finished box.

Pencil Case

This project represents one of the many uses for boxes and booklets. Using common materials, you will construct an object that is quite different from those made before.

Since it has an elastic band as a closure, it can also be used as a case to hold pencils, pens, and many other small objects.

1- Cardboard, fabric, and painted paper are the basic materials for constructing this object.

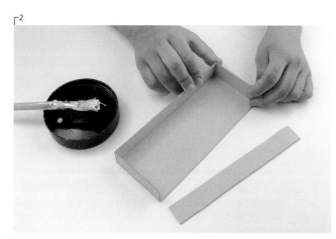

2- Over a base of specific dimensions make side pieces that are only a few inches high. Two of them are as long as the base; the other two are the same width as the base minus the thickness of two boards. This will allow perfect assembly.

3- When the cardboard pieces have been cut, cut and mount the fabric (see pages 108 to 111).

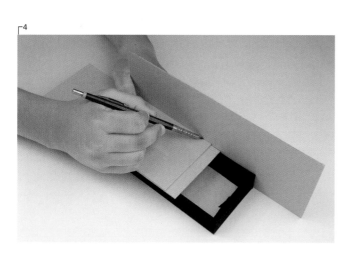

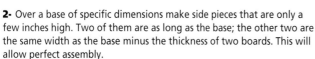

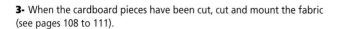

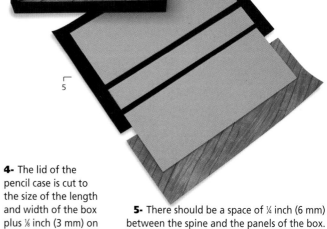

4- The lid of the pencil case is cut to the size of the length and width of the box plus ⅛ inch (3 mm) on each side, that is, ¼ inch (6 mm) all together.

5- There should be a space of ¼ inch (6 mm) between the spine and the panels of the box. This is enough to ensure that the overhang on the front is the same as on the head and tail when the piece is finished.

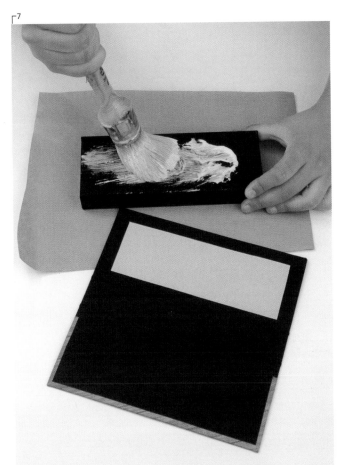

6- First, glue the black paper that will hold the panels and the spine together. Once this is mounted, adhere the painted paper in such way that it overlaps the black one slightly.

7- Glue a pastedown paper on the inside that covers the entire panel, the spine, and part of the second panel. Glue the box on the underside and place it over the lid making sure that there is the same margin around all three sides, and that when closed, the spine will fit inside the box at a 90-degree angle.

8- Make two holes with a punch on the outer corners of the upper panel. A couple of grommets will give the clean finish to the holes through which the elastic will be inserted. Make a knot with the elastic to hold it in place.

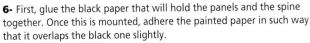

9- The finished piece with the elastic band as closure.

Picture Frame

People always like to set pictures apart for themselves or to give them to people as gifts. This piece, even though it is not luxurious, is meant to complement and enhance a proud possession. Despite having a stand in the back to keep it upright on a surface, it can be hung by attaching to it a simple hanger available in any store.

1- A 3½ × 4¾ inch (9 × 12 cm) photograph, fabric or paper to make the frame, and medium weight cardboard.

2- Cut two boards that are larger than the photograph by 1 to 1½ inches (3 to 4 cm) on each side. Make an opening somewhat smaller than the photograph on one of the panels to create the frame. Also, cut three strips of cardboard, which mounts to the panel that has no hole to let the picture slip through tightly, and glue them to it.

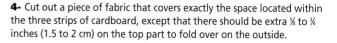

3- Now, using a rasp, file the outer part of the board on the panel with the window. To do this, place this board on top of a larger one, against the edge of the table. Then, finish sanding with sandpaper fitted on a wood piece. The sanding does not have to be too pronounced, but it does have to give the edge the feeling of being cushioned.

4- Cut out a piece of fabric that covers exactly the space located within the three strips of cardboard, except that there should be extra ⅝ to ¾ inches (1.5 to 2 cm) on the top part to fold over on the outside.

5- Take the panel where you had cut out a window and line it at an angle, leaving the outer part unfolded. Apply glue to the three cardboard pieces and attach the two units. When it is dry apply glue to the fabric and adhere it by folding it over the back side.

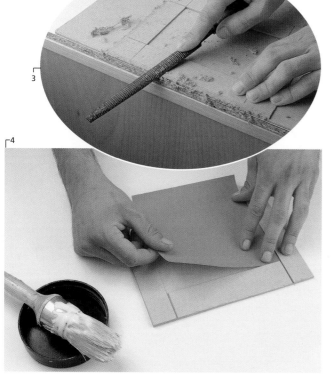

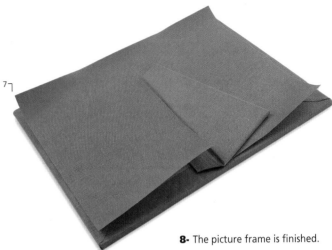

6- Now you have a picture frame that only needs the back and the stand. The back side is only a piece of fabric cut to size; the stand, on the other hand, should have a triangular piece of cardboard, which will be covered with the same fabric. Leave the fabric on the part that does not form a 90-degree angle unfolded.

7- Make a cut in the fabric on the back side and glue the folded part of the stand inside. Glue all the fabric and adjust the stand as needed.

8- The picture frame is finished.

Magazine Holder

This simple box holds magazines that you want to save or to store vertically without going as far as having them bound.

It can be placed on the shelf next to the other books and will hold the magazines in place so that they do not fall and slip as is often the case. Its design allows the magazines to be stored and removed very easily.

1- Here are the magazines, cardboard, and papers for constructing the panels and the sides of the magazine holder.

2- First, take several pieces of cardboard that are somewhat larger than needed, and line them with fabric or paper only on one side. This will become the inside of the magazine holder.

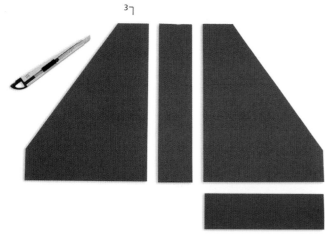

3- Then adjust the pieces to size. Begin by cutting the two side pieces, which must be as wide as the thickness of the magazines. The cut, as far as the length is concerned, is left for later. The panels are two rectangles that must have the same dimensions as the magazines plus the thickness of one board. After being cut to size, make an angled cut similar to the one in the photograph. You only need to adjust the length of the sides. To do this, cut the small one to the size of the base, while the larger one should have the height of the panels minus the thickness of one board.

4- Assemble the sides on one of the panels, and then glue the other panel over it.

5- The pieces of fabric for lining the exterior should be ⅝ inch (1.5 cm) larger on each side than the holder itself. Once these are glued, fold them inward and make the cuts shown in the picture.

6- When both panels are mounted, cut the strips that will line the sides. These should fold inward ⅝ inch (1.5 cm), the same way as the panels, and their width should be the same as the mouth of the holder.

7- The shape of this magazine holder makes it a practical device to hold magazines upright.

CD Holder

This piece is easy to make with a little bit of imagination. The design that has been chosen is optional because it can be changed according to your particular needs.

In this case, we have decided to make it in an X shape so the CDs can be stored inside, as well as on top of the structure.

1- Cut twelve 12 × 6 inch (30 × 15 cm) strips from heavy cardboard. You should have paper or fabric to line them. In this case, we suggest working with painted paper, this way the joints will not be visible.

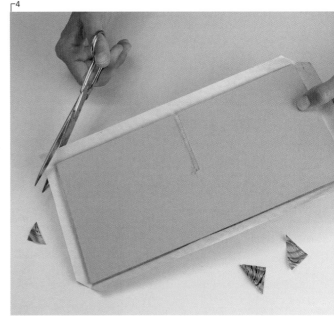

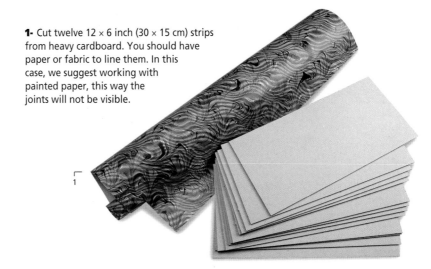

2- Glue the boards in pairs to give them enough strength. Apply glue on both of them to prevent them from buckling. Attach the pieces facing each other and place them under the press until they are dry.

3- After they are dry, make a cut in the center of the boards with a craft knife and a ruler. It should be as wide as the thickness of the two boards put together, and as long as half the width of the boards.

4- Line the boards only on one side, and cut off the tips of the paper to make folding it inward easier.

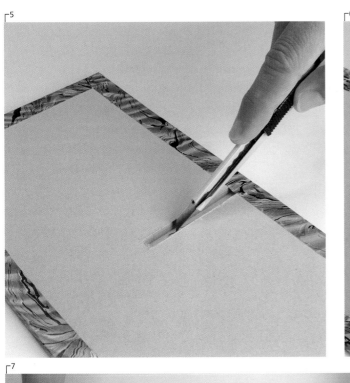

5- Taking advantage while the paper is still wet from the glue, cut it in the center and then glue it on both sides of the cut. If the paper has dried out, you will still cut it the same way and apply a little more glue with a small brush.

6- This is how the paper is tucked inside the cut with the bone folder.

7- Line the back of the board as well, leaving ⅟₁₆ to ⅛ inch (2 to 3 mm) from the edge of the paper to the edge of the board.

8- Make another cut through the paper and adjust it with the bone folder.

9- This is how the boards are attached through their central notch.

10- Once all the boards are assembled, you will have three X-shaped modules.

11- Glue the edges with rubber cement forming a single piece with the three previously made modules.

12- Reinforce the edges with a few strips of paper. Here we use white glue because it is the easiest to handle.

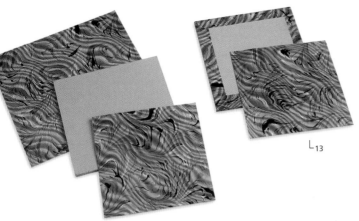

└13

13- Cut two squares out of cardboard to the size of the interior squares formed between the assembled modules, and line them with the same paper.

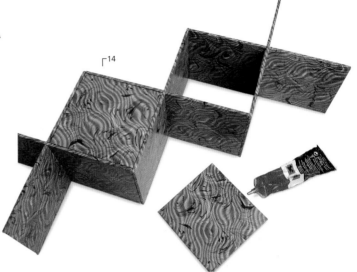

┌14

14- Apply rubber cement and glue the squares as shown in the picture. This step greatly reinforces the structure so that it can withstand the weight of the CDs for which it was designed.

15- The finished piece.

┌15

Puzzle

By choosing a specific picture and making a puzzle out of it, you transform a simple game into something personal, whether you make it for yourself or give it as a gift.

The complexity of the structure and of the case makes this a good practice exercise, while it enhances the puzzle itself with all the protective pieces.

1- To make this game, use two different color fabrics, cardboard, and an illustration, in this case the page of a calendar.

2- As a support for the illustration use a piece of heavy cardboard glued on both sides. Glue the drawing on one side and on the other a piece of paper of similar weight to counteract the pulling effect of the first one. This way the piece will stay completely flat when it dries. At that point, file the edges with a craft knife or with a rasp.

3- Make a small tray out of cardboard that will become the support for the puzzle. The walls, which act as a frame, must be thin but a little bit thicker than the board that supports the illustration.

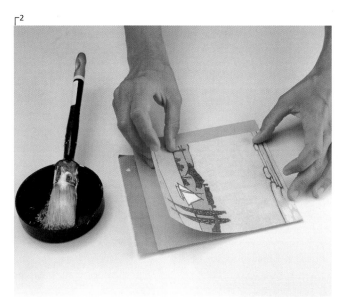

4- Once the frame has been assembled, glue on the piece of fabric that has been cut approximately ⅝ inch (1.5 cm) larger on each side than the frame.

5- When the fabric has been glued on and without moving it from the worktable, place the tray over it, in such way that the little cardboard pieces that form the frame make contact with the glue. Trim off the edges of the fabric at the corners and fold the fabric toward the middle, which will be lined later.

6- While the glue on the fabric is still wet, cut with a craft knife and attach the borders to the frame with a bone folder.

7- With a piece of fabric cut to size cover the cuts that you have made. Proceed the same way with the back area.

8- You need to construct a second tray to hold the first one. The new tray will be a little bit thicker, approximately the thickness of one and a half boards.

9- This is the way to cut the edges of the fabric to line the second tray.

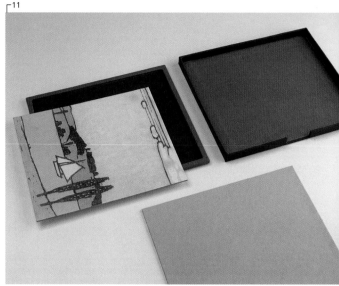

10- First, fold in the sides that need to have the corners tucked in (see pages 110 to 111), then fold the others.

11- You already have the illustration, the support for it, a second tray, which will be the base of the box that will hold it, and a piece of board to protect the illustration inside. What is left is the lid.

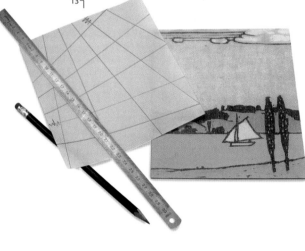

12- The lid is a third tray, which will hold everything else. You only have to place this piece upside down to function as a lid.

13- Take a piece of paper that has been previously cut to the size of the illustration and draw on it the lines that will diagram the cuts to make the small puzzle pieces.

14- Place it over the illustration to begin cutting the pieces with a ruler and a craft knife. It is not a good idea to apply too much pressure; it would be better to go over the same line gently several times than once really hard because it is easy to get off track.

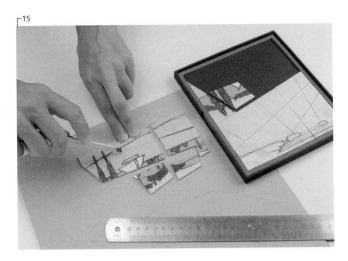

15- Separate the pieces with the craft knife as you cut them and place them carefully in the tray.

16- Insert the tray in the base of the box; cover it with the board and the remaining box. You can decorate it inside or outside with a cut out or glued on design, or both.

17- View of the finished puzzle.

Glossary

Awl

A metal tool resembling a large needle. It is normally attached to a wood handle and is used to make holes by pressing on soft materials like paper or cardboard.

Batting

Filler that is inserted between the board and the fabric of a book, to give it a padded appearance.

Bias cut

A type of cut made at the head and tail areas of the book, near the spine.

Bone folder

A tool made out of bone, wood, or some other material that is used to fold and cut paper. It is also the most commonly used tool in the bookbinding process.

Burnish (to)

To polish or shine something using friction. For example, book pastedowns are burnished, as are edges of a cover. The ideal tool for this is a burnisher, but a cotton cloth or a spoon can also be used.

Chain knot

A series of knots that are made through all the sheets of the book, over the creases of the head and tail. They reinforce each book horizontally.

Clearance

The free space between the bed and the blade of a guillotine or a shear.

Corners

Reinforcements, usually triangular in shape, that are placed on the corners of the book's cover, both on its front and back sides. They are usually made of the same material as the spine.

Edge

The edges of the pages of a book. They are more specifically referred to as the top edge, the fore edge, and the bottom edge.

Fold (to)

The act of folding the sheets of paper in half once they are cut to the desired size.

Frayed

Describes the edges of papers or books that have not been cut with a craft knife or a guillotine, thus forming an uneven edge.

Half pipe

Curvature formed by the pages of a book on the spine and front part when it has been rounded.

Head

The upper part of a book or booklet.

Headband

A piece that is placed on the upper and lower ends of a book's spine, extending beyond the pages. It can serve as an ornament and as reinforcement at the same time. It is available in different colors and materials.

Interlining

Thermal adhesive fabric that can be attached to another material to reinforce and strengthen it.

Joint

Name for the space between the edge of the cardboard cover and the cardboard of the spine, in the shape of a vertical channel.

Lining

A sheet of paper that is used to cover books to make them stronger. The term lining also refers to the hollow that is constructed with a strip of paper folded lengthwise and then attached to the spine and the covers of the book. It creates a gap or hollow area on the spine that allows the book to open flat.

Overhang

Part of the bookcover that extends beyond the pages on the upper, lower, and front parts.

Pad (to)

The act of inserting a layer of soft material, like foam or cotton, between the cardboard for the cover and the material that lines it. The idea is to make it soft to the touch. It is normally used on photo albums, agendas, and so on.

Page

Each one of the faces of a sheet of paper.

Panels

The outside surfaces of a book or a case. In a quarter binding, it refers only to the surface that is not lined by the fabric that covers the spine.

Pastedowns

Sheets of paper that are attached to the first and last signatures, and that in turn are glued to the insides of the covers once the book is completed.

Percale

A finely woven fabric, glossy on one side, that is used to make hand-held fans. In bookbinding, it is used to reinforce the sewn area and the spine in general.

Plough

A manual press with a blade that is used to trim the edges of books. This was the only way the edges were trimmed until the invention of the guillotine in the nineteenth century.

Punch

A cylindrical metal tool with a hollow tip and sharp edges that is used to make holes in paper, cardboard, and other soft materials.

Rasp

Heavy file for sanding in woodworking. In bookbinding, it is used for filing the edges of the cardboard.

Reinforcement

A piece of paper that can be glued inside book covers to keep them from warping.

Riser

A piece of cardboard or paper whose role it is to raise the level of the spine or the covers of a book. For example, risers are necessary with photo albums to give the spine the height needed for the photographs that are stored it in.

Sheet

One of the many identical parts that form a book or signature. Each sheet has two faces or pages.

Signature

Several sheets of paper of similar size that are folded in half. A book or a booklet can have several signatures.

Spine

The part of the book that is bound. We can use the term to refer to the spine of the sheets, and also to the spine of the book's cover. It can be flat or round.

Spine rounding form

Device made out of wood equipped with half-round channels of different sizes. It is used to give the curved shape to the book's spine.

Tail

The bottom edge of a book or signature.

Trimming

The act of evening the pages of a book along one edge (e.g., top edge, fore edge)

Water marks

Unique marks embedded in the paper at the time of its production.

Weight

The weight of a sheet of paper, which is often expressed in pounds. The heavier the paper the higher the number of pounds. The same type of paper can be sold in different weights, from thin paper to heavy cardboard.

ACKNOWLEDGMENTS

I would like to thank Pilar Estrada for her invaluable help and support from the onset of this project.

Ramon Serra for taking on the sections on history and painting paper.

Thanks to everyone who has lent a hand in the execution of the step-by-step exercises, especially to Trini, Marta, and Jordi Cambras, Conchita Aldonza, Mariano García, Nina Soto, and Pilar Estrada.

My gratitude also to l'Escola d'Arts i Oficis of the Diputación of Barcelona, and to the bookbinding students whose wishes and requests, at the time, gave way to some of the objects represented in this book.

Thanks to Miquel Monedero, who for many years shared this teaching career with me.

To Georgina Aspa and Jordi Catafal, colleagues at the department Artes del Libro of the said school.

To Joan Soto, for his good eye, his opinions always on the mark, his kind friendship, and his photographic sensibility, which can be seen in this book.

To the entire group of professionals at Parramón Ediciones, especially its editor in chief María Fernanda Canal, for her confidence in me for this project, for her enthusiasm, and for all the support that I have received from her.

Finally, I thank my wife Carme for her unconditional support and her patience at all times.

And to my parents Gaspar and Maria Dolors, who are responsible for my finding this profession.

Josep Cambras

BOOKBINDING

Project and realization by Parramón Ediciones, S.A.

Translation from the Spanish: Michael Brunelle and Beatriz Cortabarria

Original title of the book in Spanish: *Tecnicas Decorativas: Encuadernacion*
© Parramón Ediciónes, S.A., Primera edición: Septiembre 2006
Published by Parramón Ediciónes, S.A.
Barcelona, Spain - World Rights

Text: Josep Cambras, Ramon Serra (History)
Exercises: Josep Cambras, Marta Cambras
Photography: Nos & Soto

Translated from the Spanish by Michael Brunelle and Beatriz Cortabarria

ISBN-13: 987-0-7641-6084-4
ISBN-10: 0-7641-6084-2

Library of Congress Catalog Card No.: 2007924989

Printed in Spain
9 8 7 6 5 4 3 2